My NOT-SO-CHRISTIAN Walk with The Holy Spirit

Dina Harris

First Edition

Fulton Books
Meadville, PA

Published by Fulton Books 2023

ISBN 979-8-88731-537-9 (paperback)
ISBN 979-8-88731-538-6 (digital)

Printed in the United States of America

This is the story of my *not*-so-Christian walk with the Holy Spirit. When I first started writing down the insanity that was happening in my life, it wasn't long before I realized that I had been focusing on all the wrong things. I had been focusing on all the hurt and pain and how much I had been wronged by the people I had trusted and loved, not to mention the complete disaster I had been making of my life once again with my addictions. What I started to see as I was writing down my story is how God was working in my life. I'm a little slow but, slowly but surely, I began to see how the Holy Spirit God had gifted me with had been working things out for my good, despite myself, and at the same time, teaching me that I was on the wrong path of who he had created me to be.

I am a woman of mature age; in other words, I'm old enough to know better!

It's the summer of 2022, and I find myself renting a room from an extreme alcoholic in California, and how I got myself here is part of the insanity I had created for myself with drugs and alcohol and a narcissistic relationship I was trying to escape from. I found myself over 250 miles away from where I was living and renting a room in exchange for housekeeping from a man who drank like a fish and sold marijuana, so I had an endless supply of pot and alcohol. The house itself was surrounded by angels, inside and outside of the home, and the actual owner of the home was his mother who had just passed away. This woman was an artist and had surrounded herself and her home with angels—it was as if God had directed me here because of the battle I was engaged in and fighting with the devil and a demonic narcissist, and not to mention my own inner demons. I didn't notice all the angels at first, but it all started to make sense as to how and why I ended up here in this particular place. I started to feel a sense of peace, and I don't think it was a coincidence—not now, not anymore—not after the battle I was experiencing with the devil firsthand to get me to where I am today, writing this book to tell my story. It's not exactly how I had planned my life. If you noticed, I used the word *I/me/myself*. I knew, despite my brokenness and my own inner demons, I wanted to live my life feeding the homeless and being God's hands and feet, and the devil wasn't having any of that.

The Connection

I was fifteen years old and in high school when I first experienced the Holy Spirit, and I didn't even know it. I was in the tenth grade and ditching my scheduled class to walk off campus to smoke some pot, and it was something I had done on a regular basis, but this day, I walked by a classroom that was jam-packed and had standing room only. I, of course, was very curious and tried to sneak in to see what was going on, so I stood by the door trying to blend in because I didn't want to get caught ditching my class. I wasn't sure what the topic of conversation was so I was a little confused, but it was time for the next person to speak, and when he stood up he looked directly at me, and what he began to say was, "There are people here that were not supposed to be here, but they were called here by the Holy Spirit."

Just then, it was if I had just been hit by a huge wave with no water—that's the best way I can describe it. I felt extremely overwhelmed and weak at the knees. I stayed behind to see who these men were that had just convicted me with what I know now to be my Holy Spirit. What I discovered is they were a group of men that found God while doing time in prison and went around touring high schools to share their story. At the time, I was still oblivious as to what I had just occurred within me; all I knew was that I felt differently and I didn't want to smoke pot anymore.

At the time, I was the oldest of three kids and the firstborn grandchild living with my grandparents. My parents were in the process of getting a divorce, and I was sent to live with my dad's parents in a nice, stable home on the good side of town, and my two brothers had to live with my mom's mom on the other side of town, in a not-so-good neighborhood. My uncles were dealing heroin out of my grandmother's house, and my grandfather had passed away from cirrhosis of the liver, so it wasn't a very good environment for my little brothers. My mother married at the age of fourteen years old and had me at the age of fifteen, and by the age of twenty-two, she already had three kids and suffered from mental and emotional disorders and a severe alcoholic.

Blood Sisters

I needed to find a job and still go to school while living with my grandparents so I found a part-time job working fast food at night, and that was when I met Sharon. We were both working the night shift and attending high school—I went to a public school, and she attended a private Catholic high school—and it wasn't long before we became best friends and blood sisters. That was what kids were doing back in those days, and it was no surprise how stupid that was. Little did I know that would somehow create a very strong bond between us, stronger than I knew at the time; we thought we were cool, since all the kids were doing it.

Sharon's parents were not very happy we were friends; they thought I wasn't good enough to be her friend. Her stepdad was a police officer and owned a small hamburger stand in the middle of town, and her mother worked there part-time. During the summer, Sharon would work for her stepdad part-time at the hamburger stand with her mother. I went to visit Sharon one day when her mother wasn't there, and we were outside talking when I saw a speeding car pulling into the parking lot and almost hit me. I jumped on top of a picnic table from a standstill to avoid being hit by the car, and when I saw the driver, it was Sharon's mother behind the wheel of the car. Who knew I had the reflexes of a gazelle? Certainly not me. I think God lifted me up that day to avoid being run over. Sharon screamed at her mother to stop, and as she found a place to park, I quickly left the property. I could overhear Sharon yelling at her mother for almost running me over with her car, and her mom was just laughing.

One night, while we were both at work, I was not having a good day and feeling overwhelmed with the thought of being molested by my mother's boyfriend when I would go to visit my mom. I had confided in Sharon that night at work, and I told her I didn't want to hang out with her as much anymore. I was tired of the drama with her parents not liking me and everything I was going through with my mom's boyfriend, and Sharon was also getting extremely possessive of our friendship. I just needed a break.

After about a week, one night after work, I was going to hang out with someone else after work and Sharon became very upset and started to cry. She asked if I could talk to her in the bathroom for a minute before leaving work, so of course I did. She was crying and told me that her stepdad had attempted to rape her while on an overnight trip in a hotel room. I spent the rest of the night consoling her after work, and after that night, we became inseparable.

Looking back and in writing my story, I know now that the trauma she endured wasn't with her stepfather but was with her real father and she couldn't be honest about it. Her real father was also a police officer and had been shot and killed in the line of duty on her tenth birthday, and the police department he worked for placed a statue honoring his memory in front of their police station. Sharon's mother divorced her father when she was six years old, and he remarried a woman who coincidentally had a six-year-old daughter also, so Sharon and the little girl were both ten years old at the time of his death.

Sharon and I were extremely close, and in all that time, she never once told me anything about her father, not one fond moment with him in ten years. What she told me was, he had changed his last name after the military and that he was a cop who had been shot and killed in the line of duty on a domestic violence call. At the time, I didn't make much of it, but it's all beginning to make sense. The Tustin police department made a hero out of him when she was ten years old, so how could she possible tell anyone what he had done to her? I'm guessing she couldn't hold it in any longer, so she decided to blame her stepfather to share her secret with me.

Sharon was a little awkward growing up, and it was hard for her to make friends. She had a boyfriend, one friend in high school, and me. I also had a boyfriend, but the relationship between her and I was getting vey exclusive; she didn't want me hanging out with anyone without her. Her parents were very racist against Hispanics, so I wasn't welcomed in their home, but that didn't stop us from hanging out after work and smoking a little pot.

Pool Party

One weekend, Sharon invited me to a swimming pool party at her parents' friend's house. I was skeptical and really had no desire to be around her family, but she assured me that it was okay with her parents if I went. We got there and I immediately went out back to where the pool was while she was inside talking with her parents. As I was overlooking all the kids playing in the pool, I noticed a tuft of hair floating on top of the pool, and attached to it were these big eyeballs, and I could see that this little boy was in trouble; he was trying to grasp for air, so I immediately jumped in with all my clothes on and pulled him out. The adults were in the house drinking, and when I pulled him from the pool, they all came outside, very frantic. The little boy who as drowning was Sharon's little brother, and I had just saved his life. You would think that after that incident Sharon's parents would like me now, right? Uh, nope! Sharon did, however, find that to be a good opportunity to ask them if I could spend the night in the mobile home they had parked in the driveway, and they said okay.

That night, Sharon decided to sleep in the mobile home with me. After Sharon brought in the pillows and blankets for us to have a sleepover, we talked for half the night, and that was when it happened—we had our first kiss. I remember crying after that because I wasn't sure that was the right thing to do, but I had a lot of feelings for her, and back in those days, being lesbian was a big no-no and a disgrace to one's family, especially if you were in a Catholic family, like we were growing up, not to mention not very socially acceptable in the late '70s.

I was having problems at my grandparents' house because I was caught smoking pot, and my grandmother didn't play around when it came to drugs, after two days I went and stayed with a very nice couple that were friends of Sharon's parents for a few weeks. Sharon would spend the night on a regular basis, and it started becoming very obvious to her mother that the friendship we were developing was becoming very unhealthy for two girls to spend so much time together.

A Fly on the Wall

Sharon's mother figured out that we were more than just friends and that we were having a sexual relationship, and boy, did things hit the fan. I was no longer able to stay at their friend's house, but thankfully for me, I was able to go back to my grandparents' house after a few weeks. They were worried about me and they let me come home, but that lasted only a short time because once I got settled in, it was only a few short days before Sharon's aunt decided to storm into my grandparents' house without knocking—after she, herself, found out about our relationship—and chose to inform my very Catholic Hispanic grandmother that I was gay and I had converted her innocent niece. Yeah, right. Now, remember, this took place in the late '70s, early '80s, so as you can imagine, that did not go over very well with my grandmother.

I wasn't home at the time, but boy, I wish I could have been a fly on the wall that day because my aunt who also lived with my grandparents walked out of her bedroom to see what all the yelling was about. What she saw was a total stranger yelling at my grandmother about me and what I had done with her niece. I'm glad I wasn't home at the time because I know my grandmother would have asked me about the situation, one belt stroke at a time with every word that came out of her mouth, and that would have hurt.

My aunt proceeded to throw Sharon's aunt out of the house, and things got a little messy for me after that. I was kicked out once again, and Sharon had been kicked out of her parents' house as well. But since we both had part-time jobs, we had saved enough money to rent a room for a month over in the next town. I couldn't keep the job I had living at my grandparents' house because I didn't have a car, I managed to get another nighttime job working fast food within somewhat of a walking distance of the new place.

One night after work, I was walking home and I was approached by a guy in a car, and he stopped and asked me if I needed a ride home. I told him no and continued walking. He kept driving slowly as I walked, then pulled away. After a couple of minutes, he pulled up again, and this time, he told me that when he was driving away, he saw that there were two guys following me, and he wanted to make sure I got home safe. I looked behind me, but I didn't see anyone, and in that time, he asked if I wanted to smoke a joint with him. All of my common sense went out the window and I jumped into his car, and he lit up a joint and we started driving.

I noticed he wasn't going toward where I lived, so I kept asking him where he was taking me, and all he said was, "You'll see." I noticed we were driving into a park, and it was very dark. He stopped and parked the car behind a building. I was extremely scared and with good reason.

He grabbed me by my hair and began slapping me. He opened my door and pushed me out, and before I could get up, he was right out after me. He then slapped me so hard I fell on the ground, and that was when he grabbed me by both my breasts and slammed me on the ground. He did this about three or four times, and that's when I pretended to be knocked unconscious so he would stop treating me like a rag doll. I was tired of the beating he was giving me, and it worked.

He then grabbed my hair and dragged me behind some trees where he then proceeded to rip my pants off, and fortunately for me, he ripped them completely off and didn't leave them wrapped around my ankles. He pushed his fingers inside of me a couple of times, and just before he could get on top of me to rape me, there were car headlights coming into the park, and when he turned back to see what it was, I kicked him as hard as I could and he fell over. Had he left my pants around my ankles, I would have not been able to do that. Thank God for small miracles.

I got up and started to run toward the lights. The car had stopped when they noticed me running toward them. He rolled down the passenger window, and I jumped in. I had been beaten up pretty badly, and he offered to drive me to the emergency room. I was very lucky to have not gone from the flames into the fire with jumping into another stranger's car.

I asked the guy driving me to the hospital to try and get the license plate number of the other car. I didn't want that guy to get away with what he had just done to me, but I don't think this person wanted to get involved with the police. He wound up just taking me to the emergency room, and once I got to the hospital and got cleaned up, I was able to call Sharon to come pick me up and take me home.

The next day, I wanted to call my family and let them know what had just happened to me, and when my grandmother answered the phone, I told her that I had been beaten up and almost raped, and described what I went through, and her response was, "At least it was with a man."

Wow, that comment hurt more than the attempted rape! I didn't go to work that day and that night, and when Sharon came home, she insisted we have sex. Are you kidding me? I was in no condition physically or emotionally, but she wanted to make sure I wasn't damaged and I was still able to have sex with her. So I got very drunk and just let her do what she wanted to. I don't remember what happened after that; I just blocked it out. I just wanted to move forward and forget things ever happened.

At the time, I kinda still had a boyfriend, but he didn't know anything about my relationship with Sharon. He thought we were just best friends, and we only saw each other from time to time, anyway, so I just didn't feel the need to get into all the details. But after I told him what had happened to me in the park as I was walking home from work, he was very upset. He had enlisted in the military, and before he left, he gave me his car while he went to boot camp. He didn't want me walking home from work at night anymore.

Soon after, I had gotten word that my younger brother was taken to foster care because of the drugs my uncle was selling out of the house. I tried to visit him one day, and they wouldn't let me see my own brother. It was heartbreaking to see him crying from the living room window as I walked back to my car. I needed to do something. So the next day, Sharon and I went back to that foster care home, and I took my little brother from that house—you might say, I kidnapped my little brother—and took him with us. Sharon and I took him back to where we were staying and renting a room, but the owner of the house told us we couldn't have him there and that we had to leave because there were now three people in the room and the agreement was for just two people. So we found ourselves becoming homeless after that.

We packed up my boyfriend's car, a Ford Galaxy 500, with everything we owned and lived on the streets of Ventura. The plan was to wait for Sharon to turn eighteen so she would start getting survivor's benefits from her father's death benefits, which her mother had been using to pay the mortgage on her house. We all managed to live in the car for a short time, sharing seventy-five-cent burritos between the three of us and taking sponge baths in gas stations around town.

When Sharon's family found out she was living in a car, they forced her to go back home. Remember, her stepdad was a police officer, so he could have created a lot of problems for us living on the streets. It was only a couple of weeks before she turned eighteen, so she went back home, and I took my little brother back over to my grandmother's house; I just couldn't take care of him by myself living on the streets.

I slept in the car around town waiting for Sharon to turn eighteen because she swore to me as they were dragging her back home that we would be back together no matter what. The day after her birthday, she ran away and I was waiting for her in our "mobile home," otherwise known as the Galaxy 500. We packed everything we had and we were off to live in San Diego with nothing but a desire to be together, *duh*!

We lived on the streets of San Diego and sleeping in the park until we were able to start receiving the benefits from her dad, but there was a catch: we needed a physical address to start receiving the checks, and with no money, it was hard to get a place to live. Sharon smoked, so I would bum cigarettes for her on the street because she was shy. Sometimes she had ten different kinds of smokes—beggars can't be choosy, I always say!

Sex for Money

Things for two girls living on the streets in San Diego was not easy, especially when one of us was very socially awkward and it wasn't me. Sharon had a hard time making friends everywhere we went, so it was up to me to make things happen when it came to getting food and stuff.

One day, it was getting really hard to panhandle so we could eat, and that morning, I had been taking care of another homeless person that had just been beaten up and bloody. I was cleaning him up when a man came up to me and offered me $20 for sex. Sharon had been registering at the city college that afternoon, and I knew she would be hungry when she came back and want to smoke, so I told him I would. I was so scared the entire time, and all I could do was pray to God that he wouldn't kill me when he was done.

After he finished, I felt so disgusted with myself, but he did drive me back to the park and gave me the $20. He told me he had been watching me when I was bandaging up and taking care of the person who had been beaten up, and that I was different. I'm not sure what that meant, but maybe that's what kept me alive. I was able to buy alcohol, cigarettes, and something for us to eat that day—$20 dollars went a long way back in those days—and since we had a little food to share, we also made a friend who called himself Mad Dog. He decided to take us under his wing; he clearly had more experience living on the streets than we did and he was a pretty cool dude. I don't think Sharon ever knew I had sex for money that day, but I think she knew something was wrong with me because I just wasn't acting the same after that. I was feeling so dirty and disgusted with myself.

Sharon started communicating with her mother again and managed to get her to help us get an apartment so she could attend college, but one of her mother's stipulations was I couldn't live with her. Sharon agreed but lied to her mother, obviously, and we were able to get an apartment very close to the city college.

I had to finish up some high school credits. I then enrolled and took a few college classes of my own. One of my favorite classes was bowling. I didn't take school as serious as Sharon did, but she insisted I go to school, which was a good thing for me, but once she started school and she was paying for rent from her father's survivor's benefits, she became extremely controlling. When I wasn't taking any classes, she had me learn the first five books of the Bible.

The Torah

Sharon was taking classes full-time, and in the meantime, I was taking care of the apartment and not in school full time, so she insisted I study the Bible. She had me reading Genesis, Exodus, Leviticus, Numbers, and Deuteronomy, otherwise known collectively as the Torah. When she came home from school, she had prepared a written test for me to do—a page long—and would grade it for me after I had written down the answers.

I began drinking more and more while in college and still smoking marijuana, when I could find it. Sharon was becoming very aggressive and would like to wrestle with me a lot. We were both tomboys growing up, so I would engage with her while we were in bed just wrestling around, but when she had the upper hand, instead of having me tap out like they do in wrestling, she insisted I say, "White supremacy"; otherwise, she would keep hurting me. Being that she knew the Bible very well and she had me studying it, one of her jokes was, the golden rule, and that was, whoever makes the gold, makes the rules! I'm sure that's not how God intended it to be, but that's how she lived her life even back then.

As time went on, we were able to get a bigger place and moved from a studio into a one-bedroom on the other side of town. I was drinking more and more because things for me were getting out of control with Sharon trying to be controlling. I started blacking out very quickly in my drinking career.

Warning from the Holy Spirit

Sharon and I started to drink on a regular basis, and it wasn't the good stuff either. Our drink of choice was MD2020, but that was all we could afford at the time and it did the trick. We were starting to settle into our new apartment when early one morning I had a dream that her mother and aunt were walking down the hallway of our new apartment. I woke up with my heart pounding, and about five minutes later, I got up just before we heard the knock on the front door, and guess who it was? You guessed it, it was her mother and aunt at our front door. Clearly, my Holy Spirit had given me a vision.

Remember, Sharon lied to her mother and told her we were not living together, so I had to leave immediately without being seen through the backdoor and with very little clothing on. With nowhere else to go and new to the area, I really didn't know anyone and I wasn't dressed to go anywhere, so I stayed in the stairwell, not knowing how long they would be visiting.

After a couple of hours, Sharon brought me something to eat because she knew I would be around the complex somewhere and brought me a different shirt but she couldn't tell me how long they would be staying.

The downstairs neighbor had seen me early that morning in the stairwell and we said hello to each other, and after a few more hours went by, he saw me again in the lobby and struck up a conversation with me. I explained to him what was going on with Sharon's mother and aunt and how I couldn't be around them, and he was very nice about everything and he invited me to his apartment for dinner. I'm not going to lie, I was very hungry by this time and he seemed like a nice enough guy, and he was my neighbor, so I agreed to go to his apartment. He offered me a beer, and we had something to eat, and then he asked me if I wanted to have sex with him. I told him no.

He then told me, if I didn't agree to have sex with him, he would break my neck and throw me out of the second story window and tell people I jumped because I was upset. He then grabbed me by the back of my hair and took me to his bedroom and threw me on the bed, where he proceeded to rape me. As he was raping me, I could hear Sharon and her mom and aunt upstairs having dinner and laughing, carrying on a conversation. I know they had no idea what I was going through, but listening to them having a good time, I couldn't stop crying. I could hear the dining room chairs being moved around as if they were done with dinner and cleaning up. It did take my mind off of what was happening to me, but when he finished raping me, he had the nerve to tell me I could spend the night if I had nowhere to go.

I immediately put what little clothes I had on to begin with and went to the corner 7-Eleven and called the police. I met the police back at the apartment complex and told them what happened, but what I didn't know is my neighbor had been a police officer in another state and given the fact that I barely had anything on, and I know I looked a mess, they believed his story. He told the police that I went up to his apartment because I had gotten into an argument with my girlfriend and wanted to have sex with him, and afterward I felt guilty about it and I didn't want my girlfriend to find out so I made up this story of him raping me. The only injury I had was a big knot on the top of my head where he was pulling my hair, so I had no visible marks or bruises to show I was forced.

It was around midnight before I could go back home, and Sharon was oblivious to everything that had happened, and I'm gonna guess her family had left before the police got there, when I was at the 7-Eleven calling the police. I told Sharon everything that happened and she showed no emotions. Again, I had no visible bruises, so I'm not sure she believed me, and things between us got really bad; she seemed to think that it was her green light to be more controlling with me.

We continued to stay together for a few more years, drinking and fighting; it seemed to be the norm for us. On the weekends, we would go to nightclubs in Hollywood because that's where you would have to go if you were gay in the early '80s and wanted to have a good time and party without being harassed. That's where I met another woman. She looked like a young, very cute Michael J. Fox. I was very attracted to her, and honestly, by this time, I didn't want to have anything to do with men; I was afraid of them. I was with Sharon for six years, and in that time, I managed to become an alcoholic and a cocaine addict and no sign of my Holy Spirt after the first few years.

She treated me well and was not a violent person. I fell in love with her and left Sharon. Sharon would not leave us alone. She was driving all over town trying to find us, and when she did find us, she started a fight with my new girlfriend. It was very sad. I felt terrible; I didn't want to hurt anyone, but I knew I couldn't stay with Sharon because our relationship was very volatile. My new girlfriend's father was a retired colonel for the Air Force, and in order to hide from Sharon so she couldn't find us, we had to rent a small bungalow on a military base for a week so we couldn't be found. It worked, and I managed to get away from Sharon.

My girlfriend joined the Navy, and after some time, we moved to Hawaii for two years, where I got involved with drugs again and continued to battle my inner demons. Despite my alcoholism and my smoking ice, I was now the abusive one in my relationship with my new girlfriend. It's no excuse, looking back, but because that's what I knew, that's what I thought a relationship was supposed to be like. I thought that's how love worked. My new girlfriend would never raise a hand back to me. She would always say, "Big people don't hit little people," and I was smaller than she was, so she would not hit me back despite all my nonsense and violent outbursts when I got drunk.

I was working immigration security in Hawaii when I got into a car accident driving a company vehicle, and I received a large settlement. We moved to Texas, where we invested some of that money on a small piece of property in New Braunfels, and it rested on the lake, and I became pregnant with my daughter. I did manage to stop drinking during my pregnancy.

Holy Spirit Came into Action

During my pregnancy and being that my girlfriend was in the military, she got orders to Oklahoma City, Oklahoma, for air traffic control school, and I began to have terrible dreams (night terrors). We had a Golden Retriever lab mix that we brought back from Hawaii and kept me company while she was in school. I painted eyebrows on my dog with a black Sharpie to cheer me up, because every time I would talk to her she would make a funny expression with her eyes and it made me laugh. I guess you had to be there lol.

I noticed there was a church on the corner of where we lived, and I felt compelled to go there because of the nightmares I was having. So the next Sunday morning, I walked to the church and I went alone and sat on the top row in the very back—it was a very large church and had stadium seating—and once again, the Holy Spirit was communicating with me to let me know what was happening to me and why. What the pastor had to say as he stood on the pulpit hit me like a wave once again and sent shivers through out my entire body causing me to feel very weak. It was mind-boggling when he said he had been working on his sermon all week and it wasn't the one he was about to give this morning because God had put it on his heart to talk about dreams this morning because someone needed to hear about it. I couldn't believe what I was hearing because I knew that someone was me. What he said was that Satan can get to a person through their subconscious and in their dreams when they are sleeping. *Wow*! If that wasn't a hint and a half that I had the Holy Spirit in me, I don't know how much more clear the Holy Spirit could have made it.

Once I heard that, my night terrors went away, but I still wasn't getting it. Remember I said I was a little slow in the beginning and still being oblivious to the Holy Spirit within me. I knew God was communicating with me, but I just didn't know how to process it.

We moved to California after my girlfriend finished school, and I gave birth to my daughter. A week after giving birth, my mother came to visit me for a week, and she was so excited to be a grandmother, and sadly, that was the last time I saw my mom. She went back to Vegas, where she lived, and a week later, she passed away in her sleep. My mother, too, still suffered from alcoholism and when she was told by her doctor she had pneumonia and needed to go to the hospital that day, what she did was go home to continue drinking and decided to go in the next day. But the next morning, she didn't wake up and she passed away in her sleep at the age of forty-three, from bronchopneumonia.

I got very depressed but breastfeeding my daughter for six months, I didn't drink, and after that, I began to drink heavily once again. We moved back to Texas, when I started to have night terrors once again, and it wasn't until I started writing my story that I noticed the connection with my drinking and the devil entering my subconscious. It's clear to me now that living with the Holy Spirit in me and alcoholism just can't coexist.

My daughter was still very young when we moved back to Texas, and I started working in a gay bar. My girlfriend and I were not getting along very well, but we wanted to stay together for the kid's sake, she also had a little girl my little mamasita, so she bought a duplex, and we lived right next door to each other.

I met a woman in the bar I worked at who was also in the military, in the Air Force as a nuclear medicine tech. She managed to talk me into letting her adopt my six-year-old daughter so we could move to Maryland and have the military pay for the move. I was so deep into my alcoholism and not really thinking straight about who I would hurt. I was being extremely selfish as usual, and after a 10 year relationship of to Maryland we went, and the saddest thing I ever had to do was to leave my one-year-old goddaughter back in Texas. It broke my heart.

My Job at UPS

After moving to Maryland, I got a job working the night shift at a large packaging hub at UPS. I started as a loader, and only after a few weeks, I was accosted by a man working full-time for the union delivering packages. It was late, around 2:00 a.m., and I was trying to leave the building through a long hallway when, to my surprise, at the other end was this guy, and he wouldn't move out of my way and let me pass. He was blocking my exit moving from side to side so I couldn't get out, taunting me. I was so scared I didn't know what he was going to do, and fortunately someone else was trying to come in through the hallway and hit him in the back with the door and I walked out.

The next morning, I made a complaint to my supervisor, and they had me write a statement as to what occurred. It didn't do me any good because all it did was irritate the idiot, and he harassed me from that point going forward.

I sorted packages, and I did just about all the jobs the company had to offer. After about six months, I was promoted to a safety supervisor, and I took employees to the hospital if they were injured. After a couple of years, I taught a job they had newly implemented called cornerstone. It was a classroom environment for five days in package handling. As a supervisor, most of the supervisors would get together after work and drink. It became a nightly event for us alcoholic supervisors, and that's when I began having an affair with a married woman with two kids. She was my best friend, and I loved her dearly but in a friendship sorta way, but she fell in love with me, and it broke my heart that I just didn't feel the same way. I wasn't trying to convert anyone; I was just having fun and was in the throes of my alcoholism. I was drinking every night after work and not coming home till the sun came up. It wasn't enough that I was having an affair with a married woman, but I also started an affair with my boss—talk about being confused! My immediate boss was a man, but there was something about him that I was attracted to. Alcohol and drugs were clouding my judgment; I didn't know what was going on with me.

Despite my drinking problem, I had been working five years for the company and was doing very well at work. When I was asked to throw my hat in for a full-time loss prevention position with the company, I managed to get that position, and I enjoyed being part of the security team there, but in having that position I was setting myself up for a lot of unsafe situations. I once again encountered that idiot that wouldn't let me walk down that hallway when I first started working. He and his friends were involved in bullying some kid so much that he feared for his life. One night, the kid brought a gun to work, so that he wouldn't get beaten up after work. But unfortunately, what happened was, as he was being chased by the idiot and his friends after work, the young kid turned and shot the wrong person, killing him. The wrong person went to jail that night for life.

I was also asked to search for a bomb, after a bomb threat had been called into the company's dispatch, and instead of shutting down the operation and following protocol, they had me looking for the bomb in offices where the caller said it would be. Once I found what looked like the package, I didn't touch it. I just closed the door and told my immediate supervisor where it was.

I was still having an affair, but he was no longer my boss; we just worked in the same building. I became pregnant with our son. That didn't go over so well with the girlfriend I was living with, but there was no way I would get an abortion. I had my son and continued working for the company. I also continued my affair. I really loved this man, but he was married and had two kids of his own.

I went back into loss prevention right around the time the company had been intercepting threats about the Twin Towers. It started when one of the letters had accidentally ripped open, and we read threats of 9-11, so when we saw letters or packages from that same return address, we intercepted them. They weren't taken very seriously at first, so I'm not sure what we did with them, but clearly they were some type of warning that we ignored, and we all know what happened on 9/11/2001.

There was never a dull moment working the night shift. Another incident at work where my Holy Spirit saved my life is when I was at a gas station getting gas in my car so I could patrol the parking lot before the night shift let out, around 1:30 a.m. I was checking my tires for air when I heard a voice telling me to turn around, and when I did, there were two men hunched down low walking very fast, one on each side of my car attempting to grab me. I quickly dropped the air nozzle and jumped into my car. One of them grabbed my door handle and attempted to open my door; it was locked so they looked at each other, laughed, and went back to the street where they had a U-Haul parked. I was trembling with fear and I sat in my car for a couple of minutes, then I went back to patrol the parking lot at work. Thank God for my Holy Spirit that night.

The next day, I reported what happened to a police officer we had working for the company. He suggested we go back to the gas station to see if they had any video cameras. They did, but they were not working that night. That was the beginning of the end. I started really struggling with panic attacks, anxiety, and PTSD, but I really didn't have a name for what I was feeling. I just drank more to cope with what I was feeling. The straw that broke the camel's back was I had to come into work early one night to do time cards and catch up on some paperwork when I noticed a group of men playing basketball in the entrance of the building, and one of those men happened to be the idiot that had been harassing me throughout my six years of employment. I walked into the building and walked to the back where my office was, and about twenty minutes into my shift, I started to smell smoke. I got up and opened the door, and there was a fire in the outer office blocking my exit. My office was filling with smoke, so I had to climb up through the ceiling tiles that led to an outer office to call for help. There were supervisors having a meeting in another office, and one of them grabbed a fire extinguisher and put the fire out. Someone set a high-value tote on fire just outside my office door. I kept asking for someone to call the fire department so someone could investigate what had happened, but they just told me to go somewhere to calm down. They didn't want to stop the packages coming in and that would slow down the operation, so I went into another office and called the fire department myself, but by the time the fire department showed up, everything had been cleaned up by management and set outside, as if nothing had happened, so there was nothing for them to investigate. The only thing the fire chief said, that I could hear was he could smell an accelerant and that's what started the fire. They had me finish my shift, but the next day, I called the fire department to get some information, but all I got was the runaround.

It was getting more difficult for me to go to work. Just the thought of having to go into the building caused me extreme anxiety. I had been seeing a psychiatrist and taking medication for depression and anxiety because of everything I was going through at work and nothing for my panic attacks, but since I didn't stop drinking alcohol, the medication wasn't helping, anyway, and it seemed like every time I told my therapist what I was experiencing, he would prescribe another medication. I was on ten different medications within a year. One of the medications I was taking caused me to have seizure while I was driving, and I hit a parked car in my neighborhood, but I continued to drive myself to the liquor store and buy myself alcohol. I went through the drive-through with my forehead profusely bleeding. The liquor store attendant asked me why I was bleeding, and I told him I had been hit by my husband in an argument, he said, "Bummer," and continued to sell me two beers. The next thing I remember is I was taking my shirt off to stop the bleeding, then I pulled into a parking space where I passed out.

The next thing I remember is a police officer opening the driver side door when I passed out again only to find myself in a helicopter being medevacked to the trauma center, where I received thirty-two stitches in my forehead. I was slowly killing myself with pills, alcohol, and I added cocaine to the mix. My doctor took me off the pill that caused my seizure but kept me on the rest of the medication, and after a few months, I remember I looked in the mirror one day, and I didn't recognize myself. I made the decision to stop taking the medication myself—not the cocaine, not the alcohol, but the medication. I didn't like the person I was turning out to be. Really smart, I know, but I stopped taking my medication all at once, and all I remember about that decision was I laid up in my bedroom completely dark for three days drenching in sweat and my girlfriend brought in a slice of spinach, white cheese pizza.

When I told people how I stopped taking all those pills, I was told I should have been dead, but once again, I'm gonna guess God had other plans for me because I didn't die in my bedroom in those three days. When I came out of it, I stayed sober for a while, but the company I worked for placed me on workmen's comp then forced me to file for social security disability. I was very upset at the way they handled everything I had encountered at work, so I hired an attorney to try and negotiate a settlement with the company and paid him a $1,000 retainer.

The company had arranged a meeting with three men from corporate, and the night before the meeting, my attorney called me and said he couldn't make it, so I attended the 8:00 a.m. mediation alone. I did not do very well negotiating for myself against three men from corporate. My attorney was running for a political office soon after that, and that was a large company I was going up against, so I'm guessing he didn't want to make enemies with an internationally well-known shipping company.

My life was not going very well. My head was spinning out of control and so were my panic attacks, and the only way I knew how to cope with my problems was again with alcohol. My girlfriend was trying to take custody of my son because she couldn't have kids after her abortion, so she wanted to take mine, and honestly, I was no mother of the year. I was drinking every night, and when I was detoxing and she was feeding me pizza, she had convinced me to let her adopt my son, in case I didn't make it and/or if the social services would try to take my kids from me. I was not in my right mind to make a good decision, but my son was already four years old at the time, and I thought I would get my life together before things got too out of hand, but I didn't. I, once again, didn't know how to deal with all my problems except for to drink and numb them and hope they would all go away, but we all know that's not how things work. It was total insanity to continue to do the same things over and over and expecting a different result!

My girlfriend and I would get into knockdown drag-out fights over it, and one night, she stepped on my foot and pushed me backward and snapped my ankle. I actually heard it snap. I had surgery and had a metal plate put in it. She started taking out her frustrations out on my kids, especially my son. My daughter was old enough to stick up for herself, but my son wasn't, and she would constantly terrorize him. I still couldn't stop drinking—that goes to show how out of control I was. I was allowing this woman to abuse my children, and all I could do was fight her in front of my kids and continue drinking. I cringe just thinking of all the trauma my kids went through.

After a while I got another job at our local mall doing security, and that's when I met a man who would soon be my husband. We struck up a conversation over the fact that he was stationed in the town I was born and raised in, and in fact, he was there in 1962, and hey, I was born in 1962—he was twenty years my senior. we had a laugh over that, and I thought he looked really good in a uniform, and he was the only man I ever felt safe with. He knew I was in a relationship with a woman, but it didn't seem to bother him, and in a month's time, we went to the courthouse and got married. I was very impulsive when it came to making decisions, obviously.

My now ex-girlfriend hired an attorney and fought me for custody of my son. You would think I would stop drinking right? Uh, nope! Once again, things got really out of control, and I couldn't handle things, so I just drank. My son would call me at night, and we would say the Our Father over the phone. It was killing me inside and I fell into a deep depression. I felt as if my heart was being ripped from my chest. I believed in God and I still felt spiritual; I just didn't know how it all worked. The devil had me right where he wanted me and I didn't even know it.

I continued working security with my now husband, a retired Navy Seal, and I'll have to say I had some fun doing it. The mall had a dress code, so when the young guys would wear their pants halfway down their butts showing their underwear, around the mall walking like a penguin, I made them pull up their pants or they would have to leave the premises. I made a game out of it; it was hilarious.

I met another security officer who introduced me to crack cocaine, and as you can imagine, that was clearly one of the worst things I could have ever done—I was obviously not making great decisions. I was losing custody of my son, and instead of getting myself clean and sober, I was going in the opposite direction—I was digging myself a grave.

I remember one day I was going to score some drugs with a local drug dealer, and on my way back to the freeway to get home, there was a homeless man standing in the middle of the street holding a sign asking for money. When I stopped to give him some change, he started yelling at me to stay away from him and got very hostile, but it was what he was saying to me that was confusing to me at the time, He said, "No, not you. Get away from me!" and when I looked back, he was taking money from the other car and was no longer screaming. His inner demons were yelling at my Holy Spirit, that's my guess! I was struggling with my own inner demons, but somehow I still had a good heart and God was still with me holding me together.

I managed to get another DUI and spent three days in jail. At the time I had had an airline ticket to California because my grandmother had passed away, and I managed to miss her funeral. I was so disappointed in myself, so when I got out what did I do? I got drunk! I was a mess and my poor husband didn't know how to handle me.

I Lost Custody

I was spiraling out of control with drugs and alcohol once again, and that little fiasco was the last straw my ex's lawyer needed to take my son from me. And because of that, my daughter was moving to Texas in her senior year of high school because I wasn't sure if I was going to do some serious time in jail. I stopped caring about everything after that. I didn't want to feel anything anymore. I never thought of committing suicide, but I surely thought about homicide, and I won't get to much into that because clearly I didn't go through with it, she's still alive.

My husband had done five tours in Vietnam as a Navy Seal, but dealing with me was more than he could handle. The devil was playing me like a fiddle, and down to Georgia I went. After a couple of months, I had another DUI and placed on supervised probation this time. My husband had to drive me around, but I still managed to find my alcohol, and one night, I drank so much that the next morning when I went to see my probation officer, I failed the Breathalyzer test. I thought she was going to let it slide because all she said to me was, "See you next time." A week later, there was a police officer at my door taking me to jail.

This time I had a ticket to go to Texas, where my daughter was giving birth to my first grandchild. My husband had to come up with $50,000 cash bond to get me out of jail. I'm guessing the judge was getting tired of seeing my face in his courtroom for drinking and driving. My husband took out a loan against the house and bailed me out, and the car ride home was very quiet. I just wanted to crawl into a hole and die.

When we got back to the house, I opened the door and slammed myself on the couch and said, "I need a f——g drink so bad!"

And just then I felt that wave again, and I thought to myself, *What are you thinking, Dina?* I replayed in my head everything I had lost because of my drinking—my son, my grandmother's funeral, the birth of my first born grandchild, my marriage—and not to mention the destruction I was leaving behind me.

And just like that, God removed my obsession to drink. It was something I had been praying for, for a long time because I know if left to my own devices, I just couldn't do it. It had to be a power greater than myself to stop me, and I knew that. I had so much faith inside of me. I just couldn't explain it to myself, why I kept doing what I knew I shouldn't be doing, but God knew what I was made of—he's the one that made me.

I had lost my driver's license so I couldn't drive myself to church, and I started watching Joel Osteen on TV, and he would say to find a Bible-based church and put God first place, and that's exactly what I did. I stayed sober for that year and got my driver's license back, and the first thing I wanted to do was find a church. I knew God wasn't giving up on me, and I could feel it, and like I said in the beginning, I'm a little slow.

I had weekend visitations with my son, and he suggested we try what he called Peggy's church. So we went there, and when I met Peggy, she was a very kind and warm woman and she made me feel very welcomed.

I attended that church for a short time when she invited me to attend a spiritual retreat called The Walk to Emmaus. It was three days of the most inspirational, overwhelming resemblance of God's *agape* love I had ever experienced in my whole life. I was born again in those three days and I truly felt like God's little soldier. All I wanted to do going forward was to be God's hands and feet and be of service to others.

Peggy invited me to go with her to nursing homes and shut-ins and give them communion. Just spending time with them allowed me to feel so much compassion for the elderly and the homeless, and that's when I knew what God was calling me to do. God had a plan for me, I just didn't know it.

It was Jim's turn to go on The Walk, and I was so glad he did because after those three days, he came back a changed man. He, too, found God and the Holy Spirit. He would actually smile again, and it warmed my heart to see him smile again after all the damage I had done. Things were going really good with my life—I had God in my life, I wasn't drinking, I was getting my son back, and my marriage was going good. I was also being God's hands and feet, feeding the homeless and helping the elderly, feeling really good about myself. I remember driving down the road in my black SLK Convertible Mercedes Benz, thinking, *This is what happiness must feel like.* Then it happened. I heard that little voice, i.e. the devil, telling me that I could have a drink again. It had been close to four years without a drink, and that little voice was telling me that I was strong enough to have just one drink.

The First Drink Again!

I was feeling really good about life, and I thought I could really have just one drink then stop, but we alcoholics know it never works that way. It's just another way the devil takes us right back to where he wants us—in jail, mental institutions, or dead—and not being the people God has created us to be.

It wasn't long before I was right back drinking again and hiding it—or at least, I thought I was hiding it, but I know my husband knew I was drinking again and so did my son. By this time, I knew I had the Holy Spirit in me and I had been born again, but I was killing it with alcohol and I just couldn't stop *again*! The devil had his grip on me once again. A little slow just doesn't cut it anymore; I was being down right stupid!

My husband and I had signed up for a mission trip with our church to go to South Carolina, to help after a hurricane, and my son was going to take care of the house and our pets. When we returned after a week, I noticed my son had gone through my things in my spare bedroom and found my hidden alcohol and what he thought was a crack pipe, but it wasn't. I was very upset that he had violated my trust and went through all my things, and when we argued about it, he puffed his chest and decided he was leaving and not coming back. I didn't stop him; in fact, I put all his clothes in a trash bags and had him come to pick them up, that's how sick I was. My son meant the world to me and I was so happy to have him living with me again, and I would have moved a mountain for my son, but once again, I was in the throes of my addiction, and I couldn't stop drinking. He should have approached me differently about it, but he was a big seventeen and three-quarters, so he thought he was right.

Things were getting worse again for me, especially with my marriage. I was miserable but I knew even with my inner demons God had a plan for me, and I was struggling with that. I wanted to be good and do good in this world; I just could not stop drinking once again, and the inner battle between my Holy Spirit and the devil I was pouring into my body was killing me inside.

I was becoming more and more miserable and discontented about everything in life. My husband didn't know what to do for me—even I didn't know what to do for myself. I was drinking so I wouldn't feel the heartbreak and the pain of my own actions, and I was becoming very selfish and self-centered and I simply started not to care about anything again.

Twenty Years Had Passed

The devil was once again running the show for me and with my son in California attending college, living with my abusive ex-girlfriend, whom he called Momma, and my daughter living in Texas with my grandkids, I was wallowing in self-pity in Maryland and spiraling out of control. I had a crazy idea to google Sharon to see how she was doing after all these years. It had been over twenty years, and looking back at my mental condition I was in, that was totally Satan working his magic, dragging me down his path, and leading me away from God and what God had planned for me. At this point, I feel my Holy Spirit took a back seat and let that darn free will take over, and he just let me do my thing.

I didn't understand it at the time as to why she popped into my head but my Google search pulled up her father and the memorials the police department would hold every year honoring his memory. I made a phone call and she answered it, and so began my journey with Satan and his band of demons. I had no idea that my childhood friend had a family of demons residing within her, and boy, did I learn the hard way.

It was now 2019 and I was bored in my marriage, and the devil had his hand on me once again with drinking and drugs. Having communicated with Sharon, I knew that she had worked for the same company for over twenty years now and looking forward to retiring and traveling, and she wanted someone to travel with. My husband had traveled when he was in the military and had no real desire to travel but I did, so that was a big attraction for me when talking with my old friend. She had remained single for twenty-plus years, and it's amazing how time, drugs, and alcohol can make a person forget the trauma a friend had put you through at sixteen years old, but I guess that's why I drank so much—it was to forget my life.

She had invited me to come to California for a visit, and I didn't think twice about it; I hopped on a plane and off I went. When she picked me up from the airport, she was wearing a pair of jeans with holes and were extremely baggy on her, and her shirt was a ripped t-shirt with bleached stains. The reason I express in detail what she was wearing is because she claimed to have so much money, so her outfit got me very confused. I wanted to give her a couple of dollars and cook her a good meal; she looked like some of the homeless people I would help. I know now that was just a ploy to make me feel sorry for her, and it worked like a charm. As broken as I was, I still had a good heart and my Holy Spirit in the backseat.

When she brought me to her house, I had the opportunity to meet her twenty-five-year-old son, who she had by artificial insemination, and still lived at home. It wasn't long before he made mention to me that his mother had never told him she loved him or she was proud of him. I'm guessing it must have really been bothering him his whole life because the first stranger he met, he chose to share that. I kinda found that hard to believe, so the first time Sharon and I had a moment when he wasn't around, I asked her about it. She excused herself by telling me she worked a lot of hours for her company and she just didn't have any time for herself much less to praise her kid. *What!* That sounded so crazy to me. I didn't understand that at all, and that should have been a red flag for me, but once again, yeah, okay this time, I'm a lot slow.

Sharon's idea of a good time was to go to Sin City, Las Vegas, Nevada, and take her son. They would go every few months, and this time, I was invited to go with them. I, of course, drank more than I should have, and as I recall, she took me to a dispensary to buy pot. I thought that was great.

I spent a few days there, and in our conversations, she had mentioned she needed a lot of help with her aunt, and I noticed that things for her were somewhat the same. She had always been a little awkward growing up and she couldn't make friends very easily, and I could see that she needed help with socializing and in taking care of herself in general. She had mentioned to me that she was struggling with anxiety every time she would have to drive two hours to take care of her aunt—the same aunt that was instrumental in having me kicked out of my grandparents' house when I was seventeen. Her aunt was now suffering with Alzheimer's and dementia, and Sharon was the beneficiary to her estate—imagine that. Her aunt had invested in a little stock called Apple back in the day, and she was now worth quite a bit of money.

I had shared with Sharon that in Maryland, I had cared for the elderly and I had experience with Alzheimer's patients and being a caregiver. She offered me $30,000 if I would move to California and help her take care of her aunt, and I jumped at the idea. I was bored with my marriage, and my son was in California now attending college, and once again I wanted to have a relationship with my son, and in the throes of my addiction, that sounded like a great idea. Let's see, all the alcohol I could drink, free marijuana, $30,000, and my son. What could go wrong with that, right?

Wrong. There was so much wrong with that.

The Move to California

I continued to communicate with Sharon over the phone once I got back to Maryland, and things seemed pretty normal. We had usual conversations about her job, and I was helping my husband clean our church, feeling very smothered. Slowly, Sharon was telling me how much she needed my help and how sick she was getting with anxiety every week trying to take care of her aunt, so I made the decision to move to California and leave my husband. I won't forget that day, because in my husband's own way, I could tell he didn't want me to leave, and what he said was, "I'll continue to put up with your crap." I didn't have to leave, but there I was again, being extremely selfish and self-centered; it was all about me and what I wanted and I told him we didn't love each other anymore and I was leaving.

I began packing, and Sharon paid for me to move some of my antiques that I had grown fond of, and I moved to California to help her and myself—or so I thought.

When I moved in with Sharon, her twenty-five-year-old son was still living there. That seemed okay at first, but he started to get very jealous of my relationship with his mother and began to start throwing big boy tantrums. It began to get worse with him arguing with her over me being there, but they were not working on his mother anymore, and I was encouraging her to stop listening to him. He was a grown man, and he needed to start acting like one, not the toxic man-child he was acting like. Her aunt didn't remember me from when we were sixteen because of the dementia, so that worked out that I was taking care of her.

He finally moved out of the house and told his mother she was going to hell for being gay. He moved out, but that didn't stop him from creating problems for us in the house because he still had a key and would continue to come over to get his mail. He would come over to the house when we were not home and move things around. It started slowly and not very often, but I was very observant when it came to things, especially my things, but I also had a terrible memory, and when I drank, things were a little fuzzy. It wasn't until my favorite pair of shoes came up missing, along with another pair of black Nike tennis shoes with a gold stripe that I never wore. I asked Sharon if she had seen my shoes. Of course, she was clueless when it came to things like that, but I knew then that her son was coming in and out of the house without us being there.

I had been taking medication for my anxiety and depression issues, and I had made an appointment to see a physician in Santa Ana, just off of First Street, and when I drove there, I saw so many homeless people on the streets that it tugged at my heart and I felt such an overwhelming feeling to help them. I didn't have a lot of money, but I thought, *How much could it cost to make a pot of spaghetti and some garlic bread and feed them?* So that's what I did, and after a while, and a few trips, I got the reputation of "spaghetti girl." The homeless began to recognize my car and call out and point to my car as I drove by.

Things at Sharon's house were getting really crazy. I wasn't sure what was going on with her; she was getting very mean in the evening after she would finish working in her office. I wasn't sure what was going on with her. I tried everything I knew to try to have her enjoy life. I would buy things that I thought she might enjoy, but she had been extremely sheltered working from home for so long and she had not experienced life outside of her house and it was difficult to please her. I wanted to help her so bad, and I tried everything I knew how to do. I did not realize at the time that she had demons residing inside of her—I was clueless.

She and her son had made up, and he swore to his mother that he had not been coming into the house while we were not home and that I had been making it up to keep them apart. I'm guessing she believed him because she was beginning to get very hostile toward me. One day, on one of my runs to feed the homeless, I wasn't familiar with how the streets ran and I ran a stop sign, and I totaled the car I was driving. It was her aunt's car I was driving, and I could hardly walk after the accident, but what's funny is I still had a full pot of spaghetti I needed to pass out because I didn't want it to go to waste. She and her son came to the scene of the accident, and I transferred the food over to her car and we both passed it out before going back to the house. She was pissed I had just totaled the car, and she didn't care how hurt I was in the accident. I'm guessing because I gave out the food after the accident, that meant I was okay. She was extremely mean to me, and her son was egging her on constantly. I was trying to be so nice to her—cooking, cleaning, decorating the house—and her response to that was, I wasn't consistent enough, she was starting to treat me like an employee of hers or one of her children and I was neither. I could see that she was beginning to exhibit some serious problems with having a relationship, or any type of friendship—she still didn't know how. She equated money to love or what she considers love. She thought if she would buy you something, that was her way of showing she cared about you. That didn't work for me anymore. I didn't want that; I wanted kindness, not money. I had money when I lived in Maryland—maybe too much money—and I still wasn't happy. I had a void in my life that only God could fill. I didn't know it then, but I certainly know it now.

I had been communicating with Jim, my ex-husband for a while, and after the accident, and with how cruel Sharon had been treating me, I asked him if I could come back home to Maryland. He said yes, and I got on a plane back to Maryland leaving everything behind. I didn't care about anything at this point; it was all just stuff. I was learning very quickly that money can't buy happiness and neither can stuff. I made a stop in San Antonio, Texas, to visit with my daughter and grandkids before going back home.

Back to Maryland

I visited with my daughter who had been struggling with her own inner demons with drugs and hoarding. I had always thought she just didn't care about house cleaning, and she knew that when I would come to visit, which was every three months, that I would clean her house, and I always did. I didn't want my grandkids to live in that mess. This time was no different. I cleaned her house and then flew to Maryland to try again with my marriage.

Sharon thought I was just flying to Texas to visit with my daughter; she had no idea I wasn't coming back, but I was still drinking and my inner demons were raging inside of me. I was so restless and drinking out of control. I couldn't sleep, I couldn't eat, and I couldn't get Sharon out of my head.

After I left Texas, she was now aware I had no plans on coming back to California, and she was constantly calling me and begging me to come back. I was feeling terrible about the way I left and because I was still drinking, I was allowing the devil to control my thoughts and my life. I'm guessing I still had a lot to learn, and God was teaching me a lesson. God had plans for me, and as long as I was drinking and doing drugs, I couldn't fulfill his plan for my life. Since there was no whale around for me to sit in his belly for three days like Jonah, so God did it this way.

I kept trying to avoid talking with Sharon on the phone, but every time I drank, my defenses were gone and I would answer her calls. Needless to say, I felt very sorry for her, and honestly, I don't know why she was doing it to herself, but so was I, and I thought I could still help her. *What the heck is wrong with me?* I couldn't even help myself. I was pitiful and the devil had me in his grips, and I know now the Holy Spirit and the devil can't occupy the same space (i.e., me), and drinking continuously opens the door for the devil. This time, Jim wasn't feeling very comfortable with me in the house, and I think it was the aura of Satan around me, and he had no problems with me going back to California, and we were still on friendly terms.

Back to California

I thought for sure Sharon knew what she was doing was wrong and that I was really only trying to help her. I had love for her, but I knew I wasn't in love with her, and she convinced me that she wanted to take care of me the right way. She said she wanted to take care of me because I took care of her when we were younger, living on the streets in San Diego. She can be very convincing when she puts on her act.

The week I moved back, we were married—it was crazy, yeah, I know. Crazy just doesn't describe the insanity that was taking place in my head. I thought, if I married Sharon, she would see that I didn't care about her money or her aunt's money. I was convinced I could help her, and I enjoyed taking care of her aunt. I loved her aunt more than I loved her, and I was really trying hard to show her how to have fun and enjoy life, and that there was more to life than just Vegas. When I lived in Maryland I was so bored, and I thought I had missed out on so much because I hadn't traveled, when in actuality, I had been so blessed throughout my life in the things I had done. I was beginning to see that regardless of all the trauma I had endured in my life, God had still blessed me with so much, and I was just being selfish once again, and slowly, I started paying attention to the Holy Spirit and I was beginning to see the lessons I was being taught.

Sharon had purchased a car and put my name on the title. I returned to feeding the homeless and caring for her aunt, and we were falling into the same routine. And for a short time, things were going okay until her son started coming around again. I really didn't care for the way he kept trying to manipulate his mother. I knew he was a liar and a thief, and I didn't trust him and his Eddie Haskell routine. He didn't fool me one bit. He didn't like me, either, and I was okay with that. One day, he threatened to slap me in front of his mother and she just stood by not saying a word about it.

I was beginning to see that her spending money was the only way she knew how to show someone she cared, and her son would just suck it up and it was creating a lot of problems in our relationship. I would pay my own bills, and I didn't understand why she would get so angry. I could see that she was trying to make an effort to be kind because I kept telling her that it was what I wanted. I didn't want her to buy me anything, I just wanted her to be kind to me, and she really struggled with that. She just didn't know how to do that. It was mind boggling to me.

She worked from home 80 percent of the time, and she had no real interaction with regular people outside of work. The majority of her interactions were with her employees, and once again, she was starting to treat me like one. We would get into serious discussions over that. I would not like the way she would talk to me at all! She would come out of her office regularly to smoke cigarettes and to boss me around, and after a while, I just wasn't taking it anymore.

One night, I was drinking, of course, and she kept pestering me to watch a show with her, and I didn't want to. When she wanted me to sit with her to watch TV, she wouldn't allow me to look at my phone or get up for any reason. She expected me to just sit there the whole time. It was just getting ridiculous. She felt the need to control something—anything. It was becoming very obvious how she struggled in life. Instead of getting better over the years with her awkwardness, it got worse.

She was still struggling with the loss of her mother who had passed away ten years prior from cancer. I can understand feeling sad over the loss of a loved one, especially a person's mother, but it was very unhealthy for her to remember it every single day for ten years. Sharon had furnished her house with her mother's thirty-year-old sofas, dining room table, dishes—just about everything you could think of that her mother had in her house when Sharon was growing up. I really tried to help her enjoy life, but she kept telling me that I wanted to control everything. I was flabbergasted when she said that. I had no desire to control anything. I knew how she was when we were younger, and I was trying to express to her that the relationship with her son and her mother's memory were unhealthy for her to move forward in life.

My drinking continued, but slowly, I could feel a change taking place in me with the Holy Spirit. I could see that all my efforts just were not working. It seemed that she would be somewhat reasonable during the day, but when the sun went down, she would become a a different person, almost demonic.

Domestic Violence

As time went on, it was becoming more and more clear to me that something was changing within her when it got dark and the sun went down. She was becoming very demonic. Her eyes would change, and even if I were to agree to what she said, she would become very argumentative and would gas light me—I wasn't aware of that term gas lighting or narcissist for that matter, until later on in the relationship. I would try to get away from her and asked to be left alone, but she just couldn't do it. I would go into a room and lock the door, but she would just kick the door in so that after a while, the only door in the house that had a lock on it was the bathroom door.

One night, things got extremely out of hand and I was trying to get away from her, and since there were no more locks on the doors, I went into a back bedroom and proceeded to barricade myself in with large items from the room. When she pushed the door in and began to grab me, I could hear the next-door neighbors outside, so I tried to push the screen from the window out to call for help. I screamed out for them to call 911 when she grabbed me and threw me on the bed, got on top of me and began to suffocate me. Just when I thought I was going to pass out, I turned my head and bit her on the arm, and she stopped and got off me. I managed to run to the kitchen to call 911 myself. The 911 operator could hear her yelling at me and the police arrived shortly afterward.

As we were both standing outside being questioned by the police, her son showed up screaming and yelling. The neighbors hadn't called the police they called her son. Then the neighbors came outside as well, screaming and yelling at me that I didn't belong there. I was describing to one of the officers outside what had taken place and how I just wanted her to leave me alone and she wouldn't. Things got out of hand and she got violent. Two other officers were inside the house investigating the damages she had done to the house. I was covered in bruises and as the, but as the officer was taking pictures of my injuries, he didn't take pictures of all my injuries. I asked him if he needed pictures of the bruises on my chest. He said no, that he had taken enough. I was cold and trembling and asked if I could please go inside the house, but they would not allow it, they said they were still investigating things.

An hour or so had passed, and based on the evidence, I'm sure they could see that I was trying to block the bedroom door with large items, and I was not the aggressor, when they came back outside, they arrested Sharon for domestic abuse and took her to jail. They handed me a seven-day protective order and said she was not allowed back into the house for seven days and they left. I locked up the house and broke down and cried. About five minutes later, I heard a knock on the front door, so I looked to see who it was. It was a police officer, and when I opened the door, I saw Sharon's son standing behind him. The officer proceeded to tell me that Sharon's son had a key to the house so that meant he lived here, and he was coming in to sleep. *Wait, what!?*

I explained to the officer that he hadn't lived here for almost two years, and they knew that; they were just in the house investigating and there was no evidence, no clothes nothing of his, that showed he lived here. According to the officer, he said he had a key and received his mail here, that meant he lived here. I pleaded with the officer to not let him in the house because he had threatened to hit me in the past and I just had his mother arrested, not to mention I was afraid of him. Her son, standing behind the officer smiled at me, and said, "I'm afraid of you too."

The officer told me to step back, that he was coming in to stay. I was having an extreme panic attack, I threw my hands up and walked back into my bedroom and pushed a small chair I had in front of the door. Two minutes later, there was a knock on my bedroom door, and at that moment, my heart was racing so bad I thought I was going to die that night. I could feel my spirit leave my body as they entered the room, and it was as if I was watching a movie. I thought for sure these guys were going to kill me and bury my body and no one would know. The officer said Sharon's son was going to collect some of his mother's things, but he didn't take any of her clothes, or any of her medication—nothing like that. What he proceeded to take was the jewelry boxes, a piggy bank, and a bible from the closet, and the officer helped him carry those things out and left the house.

What I forgot to mention is this is the same police department that had a memorial statue of Sharon's father in front of the police station, and that's the city we lived in. She had been friends with them for at least ten plus years. I'm sure they tried everything they could to not take her to jail, but with the body cameras on, they couldn't hide the evidence, so they chose to harass me instead because I hadn't been through enough that night. I was so afraid, I couldn't sleep the entire night, and the next morning, Sharon called me and made me pick her up from jail.

I knew I was given a seven-day protective order, and she was not allowed to be back in the house, but I also knew I couldn't call the police and tell them she was home. I knew I couldn't trust them at this point, and my brain couldn't handle not one more thing—it was Jell-O—and I was an emotional wreck. Fortunately for me, Sharon was scheduled to go out of town on business the following week, and for a week, I was walking on egg shells until she left. I wasn't sure what was going to happen to me, and I was suffering from PTSD, anxiety, depression, you name it. I was afraid to get into my car and drive for fear the police would pull me over and find reason to harass me, I had anxiety every time Sharon walked into a room, and I was just feeling very helpless.

The week was over, and thank goodness, I was able to call my pastor's wife and I explained to her what had taken place. She came over to the house and we had a nice conversation and she made me feel at peace. I collected my thoughts and tried to file a complaint with the police department, at least I would have something in writing as to what that officer did. That was a joke as you can imagine; it was just ignored. I also tried to file a protective order against her son, and that, too, was ignored. It was awful.

Sharon returned after a week and my anxiety and PTSD was overwhelming, I could not get it under control. Every night—and I mean every single night—Sharon would continuously harass me. Without fail, it would start around 7:30 to 8:00 p.m. and continue until she went to bed. I couldn't eat until she went to bed because she would have me so upset. I started to look for a rehab center for PTSD and alcoholism because it was becoming just so overwhelming for me that I just couldn't function. I had a puppy that I wouldn't leave with her for fear of what she would do to my dog so that was a prerequisite of where I would go to rehab.

I found a place in Malibu that would allow me to take my puppy, and oh my goodness, that place was a joke. They were not there to help anyone; they were there to collect a pay check. It was the most despicable place I could have gone to. I stayed for a total of four days. It was just ridiculous. Who monitors these places anyway? I'm guessing no one! I was expecting to see a counselor for my trauma, but they left me alone for four days, and when I asked about seeing a counselor they told me I would have an appointment on a Monday. Monday came and went, then they said Tuesday. I saw what was going on there, and I told them I wanted to leave; they were not helping me one bit.

They told me to pack my stuff and they dropped me off at the bottom of the hill at a gas station with a dead cell phone and no medication because, I'm guessing, they didn't think I had gone through enough to get me there, so they were going to add to my trauma. I was sitting at a gas station with two suitcases and my dog, looking like a homeless person. I managed to find my cell phone charger and charged it just enough so I could call a person I knew from church. He came to pick me up, and I asked him to take me to a hotel. I didn't want to go back to Sharon's house; I was too afraid.

I was stupid enough to call her and tell her I was no longer in rehab but that I was in a hotel and I would be looking for another one to go to because I knew I needed help. She managed to call my son and told him I was in a hotel and he and a friend came looking for me. That was the last thing I wanted. I told her never to involve my son in our drama, and that was the first thing she did.

I had gone outside to walk my dog, and when I turned around to go back to my room I saw my son standing there. I had purchased a four-pack of wine and had one in my hand when he slapped it out of my hand and asked me what the f——k I thought I was doing. I blacked out after that. I don't know what he was saying to me. I could see his lips moving, but I couldn't understand the words that were coming out of his mouth. I remember seeing railroad tracks, and I found myself walking toward them.

The next thing I remember was, I was in my hotel room. A couple of hours went by, I'm guessing, because then Sharon came to the hotel room. I don't know what the heck happened because the next thing I remember is she had me to going back to her house. She can be very convincing in acting very sorrowful like I said before, and to say my brain was Jell-O is an understatement.

I was there for a couple of days and her traumatizing me just would not stop; it was getting out of control. I had purchased a small recorder from Amazon because I thought if I could let her hear what she was doing at night she could see that she was being possessed when the sun went down and how she was traumatizing me.

The Three Stooges

I had a small black neckless recorder that I wore one night, and once again, after the sun went down, we got into a serious argument. I went into the bathroom and rewound it so I could play it back for her and when I did, what I heard was my voice and the demons that were coming out of my mouth. It was as if I was being possessed with the words that were coming out of my mouth with how angry I was getting. I was being convicted with the Holy Spirit, and I thought, *Oh my goodness, I was being possessed myself with my anger and alcohol.* I didn't let Sharon hear it and I went to bed.

I took out my iPad and I went to sleep listening to thunder and rain. The next morning when I woke up, I thought to myself, *I do not want to get up*. So I reached for my iPad again to replay the sounds of the thunder and rain again, when I saw a picture of demons coming out of a woman's mouth, and it said, "Never say another bad word again." *Wait, what?*

I clicked it, and it happened to be a Bible scripture on how we would be held accountable for every word we say by God. Wow, God was communicating with me through my iPad. I called my pastor's wife, and she met me for lunch. She came right out and asked me if I thought God was talking to me through my iPad. I said, "Yes." She was a marriage therapist, and she looked at me kind of funny and calmly told me that the internet was very intrusive and could hear our conversations. The funny thing is, I never said a word about my demonic words; I only thought it, and that was what popped up on my iPad the next morning.

Things at Sharon's house were more than I could handle, and she would not leave me alone. I would literally beg her to please just leave me alone. I tried to lock myself in the shed she had in the backyard, and she threatened to call the police on me and tell them that I was trying to commit suicide. I got on my cell phone and called my pastor's wife once again to see if she could help me get out of the house because Sharon would not leave me alone. We had a member of the church I attended whose husband was a police officer for the city of Los Angeles, not the town we lived in. She asked if I would trust him to call the local police department on my behalf and let them know that I just needed help leaving the house and go to the church to get help and find a rehab. I told her that would be okay. His wife called me and asked me if I was in any danger. I told her that I wasn't in any danger but that I wanted to leave the house and Sharon wouldn't let me. She told me she would call her husband and they would try to help me.

I was still in the shed, and I noticed it got quite outside, Sharon had left the property, so I attempted to go in the house, when I noticed she had locked me out and locked my dog inside—she knew I would not leave without my dog. I got back on the phone with my pastor's wife and told her I was locked out of the house. A couple of minutes later, while I was sitting on the patio, Sharon came home and opened the sliding glass door when I heard police sirens turn on—they were waiting on the corner waiting for her come home. I just sat there thinking, *Oh my goodness, I'm in trouble now*, and I was.

The police came into the house and ordered me inside through the back door and asked me if I had any weapons, and it was all downhill from there. When I walked into the house, I put my cell phone and started recording them being there, and for the next three hours, they were attempting to arrest me on a 51–50 to put me in a mental facility for at least seventy-two hours. One of the officers asked me if I remembered him from the last time he was there, then proceeded to ask me a whole lot of really stupid questions. He asked me my address, my name, my social security number, they were trying really hard to make me lose my temper. I thought my head was going to explode with the way they were treating me and my poor dog would not stop barking.

There were three police officers in the house, and after a while, all they were doing was just staring at me as I lay on the couch, and I was picturing the three stooges. I kept telling them that they were hurting my head and if they could please just leave me alone; I wasn't in any danger, I just wanted to leave the house. The sergeant kept telling me they would be leaving soon. Yeah, right! I couldn't even close the door when I went to the bathroom. They pretended they were going to let me leave, and I went into the garage and that's when Sharon told them I had smoked some marijuana when I was sitting on the patio and I could hear her laughing with one of her police friends on the porch.

The sergeant offered to take me to the local drug-infested hotel down the street, and I politely declined. There was no way I was going to stay there.

Sharon took the opportunity to have them force me to take her name off the registration to the car she purchased; she no longer wanted to pay for the insurance. Sharon went inside the house and grabbed the title to the car and signed it, then the police forced me to sign it and told me I could now leave, three hours later. I knew God had me in the palm of his hand while I was in the garage, because the way they were acting, I knew it was not my own willpower keeping me from losing it. It was only one footprint in that garage, and it wasn't mine. I don't know how I did it, but I drove myself and my dog to a nice hotel and called the same person that picked me up from rehab. The only thing I had in mind was to get myself help, and I had no idea where I was going. I just knew I needed to find a rehab that dealt with PTSD and anxiety. I knew I couldn't function enough to drive my car so I had my friend take me to a store so I could buy some clothes and things to go into a rehab. I did some shopping and while I was waiting in line to purchase my things, the woman in front of me attempted to pet my dog and I had to explain to her that she couldn't pet him on the top of his head because he was afraid. That's when she said, "Oh, like in wolf therapy."

I asked her what that was, and she told me she worked for a rehab facility. I asked her what kind of rehab facility. She said an alcohol rehab. I said, "That's too bad. I'm looking for a PTSD rehab," because that was my main issue at the time. God was all over this because that's when she told me that the facility she worked for did dual diagnoses. I was hit by that wave again. I knew God and my Holy Spirit were working overtime this time. I told my friend who I had just met standing in line, and we both said that was God working on my behalf. I went back to the hotel room and wrote this song-what can I say? That's how my brain works.

Hear the Good News Jesus Died for you
He died for you, and you, and you
I'm feeling no hope in a department store
The devil at my feet, when Jesus opened the door
He said, "Come on, girl. You know you're not alone
So get up on your feet, you've got a long way to go
As you can clearly see, you have a job to do
So drown out the world
And leave the wolves to me
J-e-s-u-s
J-e-s-u-s
J-e-s-u-s
And Jesus is his name oh
There was a God who became a man
And Jesus is his name
J-e-s-u-s
J-e-s-u-s
J-e-s-u-s
And Jesus is his name oh

Another Rehab

I called the woman from admissions to see if they would take my insurance, and lucky for me, they did—plus $5,500—but I couldn't take my dog. But at this point, I knew I needed help, and they gave me the idea to put him in a doggy hotel. For the next three days, things were just falling into place to get me into rehab, and I was able to get all the shots my dog needed and I stopped drinking. I hadn't been drinking much anyway because alcohol wasn't having any effect on me, but I also knew I couldn't get all the things I needed to do and drink. God was doing for me what I could not do for myself and that was becoming very obvious to me.

I called my pastor's wife again, and they came to the hotel to see me off. I asked her if she could check on Sharon while I was gone because I knew she desperately needed help and she would not seek help for herself. I'm not sure why, with everything she had been doing to me and putting me through, I still wanted to help her, and I still can't explain that.

I took my dog to a doggie day care and I was told I could view him on my phone to see how he was doing, and I went into rehab. The first week went smoothly; I was at what they called the detox house, and they allowed me to eat after midnight because that's what I had grown accustomed to. I could eat only after Sharon went to sleep because of her constant harassment. After the first week, I was taken to another house, and that's when the bullying started. It was ridiculous.

Being Bullied in Rehab

The bullying started almost immediately when I got to the other house. I found out this woman had been there for over ninety days and just did not want to go home, and they put me in the same room as her and she did not want me there. What I couldn't understand is why the staff was letting her get away with her bulling me.

It was around the third night, just after curfew, and she would not turn off the television and I couldn't get to sleep. I asked her to "turn off the TV, please," and of course, she did not. So I got up and unplugged it and stood in front of the television and the shouting began. A staff member came up stairs to diffuse the situation but, continued to let her watch TV for another thirty minutes after curfew. *What!* Why do they even have rules? The next day, I was written up for waking up the other clients, and I knew then it was going to be a long stay.

The classes they held were educational for me because I learned a lot about CBT and DBT therapy, and it was very informative and helpful. However, the overeaters class the women—and only the women—had to attend was ridiculous. It was our agreement upon me entering rehab that the main reason I was there was because of the trauma, anxiety, and the PTSD I had been going through living with Sharon and the Tustin police department. I also suffered from alcoholism but was secondary at this point, and they assured me that after I had completed the program and went through the classes that they would write a statement for me as to why I was there and who and what got me to seek treatment so that when I got out, I could continue getting therapy for my issues.

After about a week of being there, I wanted to place my Bible on my nightstand, but I was told that I couldn't leave anything on my nightstand because the house was being sold and they would have potential clients walking through and things needed to stay neat. That was all fine until I noticed that the young lady sleeping in the bed next to me, slowly, over time, started putting energy rocks, images of Buddha and books on witchcraft on her nightstand. And after getting written up the first time, they told me to stay in my lane, and I didn't want to cause any more problems and complain, so when the young lady went into the closet at night to practice her witchcraft, I made sure I slept with my Bible under my pillow. I wasn't afraid of her; I just wasn't taking any chances, especially with what I was experiencing with Sharon.

Being of sober mind after a period of time, it was becoming more clear to me that I was in a battle with Sharon's evil spirits. While in rehab, I attended many twelve-step meetings, and it would drive me crazy when the young people would refer to God as a she or a rock or whatever else they chose to blaspheme God with. I just couldn't keep my mouth quiet when they did that. It was clear to me that Bill W. had no problem with God. In fact, he used God, 128 times in the Big Book—not Confucius, Mother Nature, or Buddha but God. Some people have a hard time with God, but it doesn't change the facts, because we, as alcoholics, know that alcohol is very cunning, baffling, and extremely powerful in dragging us down, and if left to our own ability, we couldn't stop drinking. We've all tried.

There was a man that shared his story, and in his story, he testified that after drinking and driving and getting into a serious car accident, he had been in a coma for three months, a breathing tube down his throat and couldn't walk. He was in the hospital for a year and a slow recovery. He was now thirty years sober and a walking-talking miracle by his own admission, and he still has the audacity to blame God for all the bad stuff in the world. Maybe God was busy making sure he could walk and talk again, who knows? I guess you can't please everyone right! I'm here to tell you if you blame God, that means you believe in God, and if you believe in God, then you must believe in the devil. God didn't bring sin into the world; the devil did—evil did. So you can't blame God for all the bad stuff. *Stop it!* God is doing for us what we obviously cannot do or are not willing to do for ourselves.

I was beginning to see how God and the Holy Spirit were working in my life once again, and it's amazing how being of a sober mind can bring such clarity as to who God has created us to be, and it's up to us to listen to your own personal Holy Spirit. God promised us a Comforter. I stayed in rehab for almost three months, and in that time, I learned that I was empathic, and I had been given the gift of decrement. I had no idea what that was, but it was becoming clear that God had a purpose for me in this life, and he was teaching me a very valuable lesson, if I were so inclined to be led by the Holy Spirit, and I was.

It was time for me to get out, and I was advised not to go back to Sharon's house because of the physical and emotional abuse and the trauma I went through, not to mention I could not trust the police department in that city. The rehab center, of course, did not write any letter or statement as to what brought me into rehab—no surprise there! It had been arranged by the counselors there that when I got out, I would stay at Sharon's aunt's house in a different town, and that would allow Sharon to get the help she needed and I would be safe.

Out of Rehab

Once I got out of rehab, the only person that could come pick me up was Sharon. While I was in rehab, we had been communicating over the phone, and she was beginning to see that she herself had some serious issues. She may have not been an alcoholic, but she was what the therapists called a dry drunk. They couldn't see what I saw when the sun went down and how her entire personality would change, so it was a little more serious than that.

On the drive to take me to her aunt's house, she refused to take me there. She insisted that she had changed and she begged me to give her another chance. She assured me that she would continue to seek help for her issues, and if I didn't go back to her house, there would be no reason for her to get the help she needed because I wouldn't be there. I really had no choice at this point, I had no place to go and I thought I was strong enough mentally and spiritually now after three months, but once again, Sharon can be very convincing, like I said before, and she had perfected the act of playing the victim and suckered me in once again, and I was convinced I could help her.

Once I was back in Sharon's house, I took her at her word to seek help for her problems, but she continued to make the excuse that she was too busy working and asked me to do it for her. She kept telling me she wanted to be with her mother. In other words, she wanted to die because her mother had been dead ten years. I found a therapist for her when she actually threatened to take her own life. She was very convincing, and I poured all my time and effort into helping her, but I started to see that it was just an act. I had never seen anything like it. I had been listening more and more to my Holy Spirit and not drinking. I continued to notice that she gradually would change come nightfall. She would pretend to not remember what she was saying or doing, so I bought more recorders and a video camera for inside the house, and with her permission, I started recording our conversations. Her son started coming in and out of the house again when we weren't home, and we got into a big argument over that. It lasted into the night, and once again she began to act demonic. Her face changed, her eyes got darkened, and I knew it was evilness that came over her, and one night I started to call out her demons because I could clearly see the transformation taking place within her. I don't know what I thought I was doing, but I was casting out demons in the name of Jesus Christ and telling them they would have to leave this house because I was a child of the Most High God and I wasn't leaving, that they would have to leave and leave this host! *Wow*, that was a very intense moment.

The next morning, I was flying to Texas to help clean my daughter's house once again and what took place once I got to her house was unbelievable. When I arrived, my son-in-law mentioned that there were funny things going on in the house that he couldn't explain.

The Fire

I may have been there maybe two hours, listening to Christian music while my grandkids and I were upstairs cleaning their room and singing along, when I started to smell smoke. I thought my son-in-law may have been cooking something downstairs, but when I called out to him to see where he was, he was cleaning the room next door.

Just then smoke started to come up from the vents downstairs. My son-in-law ran downstairs to see where the smoke was coming from, and it was coming from my room downstairs. That was the room set up for me to stay in when I would come to visit. The house was filling with smoke, and we all ran outside to call the fire department.

The fire department came and put the fire out and determined that it was a lamp that had been sitting on a window seal and had fallen over and ignited directly beneath where my grandkids and I were singing Christian songs, burning the entire wall leading up to their room. The song we were singing at that moment was "Holy Spirit You Are Welcomed Here." Coincidence? I don't think so! That sent my head into a tailspin. I didn't know if I was going crazy or what the heck was going on with me.

After a few days I flew back to California and that's when God started communicating with me through my iPad. Yeah, okay. I know it sounds crazy, but this is God we're talking about. He can communicate any way he sees fit, and for me, it was through my iPad with scriptures that would pop up out of nowhere—Lion of Judah, trailblazer, and grace for purpose. When things would pop up, they would be pertaining to what I was either thinking or what I needed to do going forward and encouraging me with what I needed to do.

It was becoming very clear to me that I needed to leave this house, her demons were stronger than I had the ability to fight because although my faith was becoming very strong, my flesh was still weak and I had a lot more to learn to make me a vessel for Christ. I made the decision that I wanted to buy a van to go on the road and feed the homeless. That's what I felt I was being called to do by God. I tried to buy a used van, and I was going to convert it so that my dog and I could live out of it when we were on the road. I had found one that I could afford and I went to buy it and fill out the paper work and test drove it. It was at night and I was given the keys to the vehicle I had driven.

The next morning, when I went to pick it up, they told me I had been given the wrong set of keys and they gave me another set. Well, they had done the old bait-and-switch on me because the van I test drove and the van I took home were two different vans. All the vans on the lot looked similar. They were all used white fleet vans, so when I noticed all the tires were different and the van number was held on with white caulk, I knew then that I had been taken advantage of and been a victim of the old bait-and-switch routine. Things were not going easy for me, especially when I made the decision to do what God was calling me to do—things got downright ugly.

I was continuing to take care of Sharon's aunt, and I really loved her very much and we became very close. It was hard for me to think about leaving her, but things in the house became worse. Instead of Sharon's demons coming out every three or four days a week, it began to happen every single night. She was no longer making the effort to try and hide what was going on inside of her; she was just letting it out. I would share with her some of the recordings I had, hoping it would help her try to stop what was happening to her at night. And one night on my iPad, what popped up was, "Are you in a narcissistic relationship?" Seriously, I had heard of the word before, but I had never encountered one until now. I had no idea that's what I was dealing with until then. It all started to come together and make sense. God had my back once again and brought it to my attention.

He taught me what I needed to learn and gave me the encouragement I needed to know, that I wasn't going crazy despite all the nonsense happening in the house. I knew it was demons in that house. But try telling someone else what is happening and what you think is going on, and it makes you sound like your elevator doesn't go all the way to the top, especially if you're drinking and doing drugs. But I was clean and sober at the time, and things with her and in the house were not changing. Her son continued to change things around in the house to make me think I was losing my mind, but I knew it was him. The only thing I didn't know was, if Sharon was part of it. The anxiety was coming back in full force and getting into my car to drive anywhere was becoming more difficult. It had subsided for a while, but when I had to deal with things changing in the house and Sharon dismissing what I knew was real, my mind just couldn't function properly, and they were using my son to help them.

Sharon had bought tickets to Hawaii while I was in rehab and she wanted me to go with her, but I did not want to go once I got out. Things between us were not going very well to say the least, so I told her no, I did not want to go, and maybe she should take her son. She literally begged me to go with her. I know it sounds hard to believe, but I had lived in Hawaii for two years, and I had no desire to take a trip with her, even if it was to Hawaii. Of course, I went and for the first three days, in the hotel room, all we did was argue. We stayed for a week then flew back, only to find that her son had put a tacker on my car and had gone through all the boxes I had been packing up, and stole my collectibles I had in two foot lockers in the garage. I had $2,000 in fake twenties I was going to use as a gag gift at Christmas, and he stole them as well—ha ha, jokes on him.

Obviously, I couldn't call the police, but what he didn't know is I had taken pictures of how I left my boxes and clothes, but when I showed his mother all the evidence I had, she still dismissed it as I was going crazy, and things got even uglier if you can imagine that. Let the gaslighting continue. Oh my goodness, there were some nights that all I could say to her is, "I don't want to be like you," and walk away. It can be so easy to treat people the way they treat you, especially when they are hurting you. I wanted to believe that Sharon didn't want to be evil because she begged me one night not let the evil spirits get her, but I could only do so much. It was up to her to fight them as well, and it was very clear that she was making no effort. But every time I would hear the recording of her begging me to not let the evil spirits get to her, it would just break my heart. God was showing me how evil a person can be, and it was up to me to walk away and turn the other cheek.

I Bought My Van

I finally bought a van and attempted to convert it into a house on wheels in Sharon's garage, but things were getting extremely difficult for me to maintain my thoughts. It was getting more difficult to function, and once again, I began to drink alcohol. I know my faith was being constantly tested by the devil, and as long as I was in that house, I was no match for what was happening to me. My mind was very weak and so was my flesh. It wasn't long before I knew I couldn't function properly again, and I began to look for another rehab and put my idea of feeding the homeless on hold just long enough to get my head on straight, again.

I was trying to find another rehab when I noticed that my iPad was being tampered with. Her son had accessed my Apple iPad that his mother bought for me and all its functions. Not only that my Apple iPhone would come up missing from time to time, and it also was acting up—someone was accessing all of my information. That explained why, when I would reach out to certain rehabs, I was getting no responses back. He would delete things and move items around through family sharing, and I know I never signed up for that. I spent an hour on the phone with Apple support to try to fix it. They did fix it for me, only to have it all back the way it was within an hour. he was really doing a number on my psyche. The backpack I had all my personal information also came up missing for about a week then returned minus my birth certificate and social security card—all my important papers and pass words had been compromised. My credit cards were being used, my Amazon account was being used, and when I tried to go to a different police department for help, I was told I had to go to the city I lived in and report it to that police department there, are you kidding me.

I was losing my mind, and there was absolutely nothing I could do about it. Sharon and her son had stolen my I phone, so I left the house without a phone. I just hopped in my van that day and left. I didn't know where I was going but I just couldn't take it anymore. I had this great idea to drive to Tijuana and have someone there fix up my van for cheap. Did I say great idea? Because that was the dumbest idea I had all day. Oh my goodness.

So I arrived in Tijuana around 3:00 a.m., and I thought I would find a beach and wait till morning. Well, I got lost and I found myself driving up hill in a…I guess you can call it a neighborhood. I knew the beach was not up a hill and I attempted to turn around, and that's when I saw a man staring at my van from his balcony. We made eye contact for about three seconds, and I about peed my pants. I was hoping this guy would not take out a gun shoot me and take my van—after all, I was in Mexico at 3:00 a.m., obviously lost.

I finally found my way to a main road but still couldn't find my way to the border and I had changed my mind and my doggie had to go to the bathroom. So I had to stop near a very dark dirt lot, praying no one would notice. The sun was coming up and it was getting easier to see what was around me, and I finally found my way back to the border heading into the US. It took me three hours to get back across, and when the border patrol asked me why I was there, I told them I wanted to have my van converted for cheap. They told me, "Don't come back," and I was very lucky to be getting out of Tijuana and still have my van.

I didn't know where I was going because I had nowhere to go, so I stayed in a very shady motel near the border, trying to get my brain to focus, but it didn't work. I wasn't drinking to get drunk; I was drinking to stop my head from racing one hundred miles a minute because I needed a plan, and without a cell phone, I was literally lost.

I had an aunt that lived in the city of Ojai which was four hours away, and I knew how to get to her house without my phone, so I decided to drive there and figure things out. Once I got to her house and I explained to her what was going on, she told me I could not stay there and she didn't want my dog in the house, so I went and stayed in a hotel.

When I got to the room, I was exhausted, emotionally, mentally, and physically, so my dog and I went to the room to take a nap. I woke up to the smell of smoke. I knew I wasn't cooking anything, and when I got out of bed, I opened the bathroom door and it was on fire. I grabbed my dog and ran out of the room. When the fire department came, they determined that the ceiling fan—that was not running or turned on—caught fire while I was sleeping, i.e. an electrical fire. Out of nowhere. Are you kidding me? Another fire!

The manager of the hotel put me into another room, and when the maid was helping me move my stuff into another room, she dropped my brand new $1,000 iPad and then refused to reimburse for it. It was just one thing after the other; Satan was not letting me catch my breath. And by the way, did I mention I was losing my mind? Because I was.

It was only one footprint in the sand at this point—God was still guiding me and I could feel it. "Feed my sheep." That's what I kept hearing in my soul, and that was what I was doing this entire time, even though I was struggling with my own mental issues. I would still make time to feed the homeless and share God's word everywhere I went, if only for a moment.

I went back to my aunt's house, and she let me stay in her garage with my dog. I went to the bank to take a $3,500 cash advance on one of my credit cards, so that I would have cash on hand because I wasn't sure where I was going after I left my aunt's house. My aunt continued to ask me what I was going to do when I left her house, and all I could say was I had faith God would bring someone or something to my life. All I had to do was trust God. She scoffed at me and said I could stay two days. I had plans with the money I took from my credit card, and I was hoping I could rent a room somewhere, but when I was leaving, I noticed the tennis racket cover I put the money in—to try to hide it—was unzipped and sitting next to her work bench in the garage. She was a few feet away smoking pot and told me I had to leave.

The Hits Just Keep on Coming

As I was packing up to leave, knowing my money was gone, I looked at my aunt and told her I was missing the money I had taken out of the bank. She gave me $150 and said, "I'm sure you'll find it."

I couldn't believe what I was going through, and I knew my faith was definitely being tested. As funny as it sounds, I felt a sense of inner peace that I can't explain. I had no place to live, no money, but I was strong on faith and my Christian music. My Christian music literally kept me alive driving through the mountains in Ojai. I never in my life thought of committing suicide in the past, but I'm going to have to admit that the thought did cross my mind to drive off the mountain side after my aunt took my money. That was Satan trying to work on my weakness, but I looked at my dog and I heard one of my favorite songs from Eminem, "I'm Not Afraid" is not a Christian song, but it helped me. I couldn't hurt my doggie. I couldn't do it. Those demons were doing jumping jacks, and I wasn't going to let them take me down, not like that, and neither was my Holy Spirit! I would listen to Christian music most of the time, but every once in a while, I needed to get mad at the devil. One of my favorite songs was Julia Brennan's "Inner demons." Plumb, Mathew West, Danny Gokey, and for King & Country—they saved my life. If it wasn't for my Christian music, I would have really lost it. It would give me the strength I needed to keep going and trusting in God.

I had met this person when I stayed at the hotel in Ojai, and he knew I was pretty much homeless. He wanted me to stay at his house and help him with his business, but I was not comfortable with that. He took me to look at a few camping spots, and I considered staying in one of those place because I knew God had a plan for me, I could feel it, I was just waiting to see what it truly was, but I knew it wasn't to live with that guy. I was still without a cell phone, and I really had no place to go so I did hang out with him for a couple of days, and he mentioned that he had a friend whose mother was a painter and had recently passed away, and he needed help cleaning her house and selling some of her paintings. I told him I would be interested in helping with that if I could stay there in exchange for rent. He hesitated in introducing me to his friend because he was trying to get me to stay with him, but he could see that I was kind of losing it. I had not been able to listen to my Christian music because we were up in the mountains, and Satan was entering my thoughts constantly.

I shared with him that I had a dream, and in that dream, I wanted to drive back to that police department that had traumatized me, pour gasoline into the fountain of Sharon's father, and set it on fire. I was really losing it, especially when I drank a little, and I could see that but I couldn't stop it. I told him I really needed a place to stay, and I would be more comfortable staying with his friend three hours away.

I met his friend and we agreed that I could stay there rent-free if I helped him clean it and sell some of his mother's paintings and antiques she had collected. This person also had a house in Mexico, and he needed to go back and handle some business and wanted me to water his marijuana plants and keep them alive while he was gone. I didn't know it at the time, but he made his money selling pot, so I had an endless supply of pot and alcohol.

After a couple of days of rest in his house and collecting my thoughts, that's when I started to notice his mother had a collection of angels throughout the house, inside and outside her house. That's when I knew God had directed me there on purpose. I knew then I needed to write my story. This was clearly the metaphorical fork in the road—do I want to follow the path my Holy Spirit was guiding me to, or do I want to continue on the destructive path with drugs and alcohol?

Here I was in a house, living with a man that drank and smoked pot all day long and he made his living selling pot and selling all the things his mother had worked hard for. I made the choice to listen the Holy Spirit and walk on the path God had intended for me. He gave us free will for a reason. God wants us to choose him. I could see looking back that I never walked alone; he was always there with me. I just needed to put down the drugs and alcohol and listen to what my heart and my inner peace was leading me to do.

The four weeks he was gone, I made a promise to God to stop drinking and doing drugs, and I started writing, I started volunteering at the food bank to feed the homeless, and I found a church. God was still encouraging me through my iPad with scripture and miracles.

God's Miracles

I didn't have a job, but I was still collecting my social security disability, and with the bills I had accumulated, I was having a hard time making ends meet, and the house I was staying at needed money to keep the electricity on. I went to a pawn shop to pawn some jewelry I had, and with the amount they said they would give me, I would still be $200 short. But when she gave me the money, I went in my car to recount it, it was $200 more than they said they gave me. I thought, *Wow, God really worked a miracle*, but I was feeling convicted by my Holy Spirit and not feeling comfortable with taking the money.

After a while of debating my feelings, I decided to take the money back. When I did, they were closed. They were closed for the next two days after that, and I needed to pay the electric bill so I gave the money to the other person renting a room to pay the bill. The first day after the pawn shop opened, I went in and explained to them that they had accidentally given me $200 more than they were supposed to, but that I had to use it, and I would be willing to work it off, sweeping or cleaning, whatever they needed me to do. They went back to check their records, and when they came back, they said they did not show they were short that amount. Okay, I explained to them again what happened, and they insisted they were not missing any money. God was showing off!

I was continuing to help feed the homeless and doing my best to be God's hands and feet. One day, when I was getting ready for church, I remember thinking I needed some perfume but I wasn't going to spend any money on it. It just wasn't that important, and again, it was just a thought. I had taken my dog to the park one day a few days later, like I did on a regular basis, and there, in the grass, was a full bottle of Victoria Secret perfume. That's usually what I wore, not that particular scent, but still, God was showing off once again. I knew I was on the right path of who God had created me to be.

The person I was renting a room from came back from Mexico, and things started getting very uncomfortable for me. He was drinking and smoking from sunup to sundown, and I thought, *Oh my goodness, is that what I acted like?*

God was once again teaching me a lesson and showing me what I was probably like when I drank too much. I thought to myself, *I so deserve living with this fool.*

I was trying to find a job because, all of a sudden, he needed me to start pay rent, and he was becoming very belligerent with me, so I knew I needed to find somewhere else to live. I was working on getting a divorce from Sharon and that also became a nightmare. I still, believe it or not, did not have a cell phone. It had been about three months without a phone, so I was just letting God lead me.

The attorney I found was an alcoholic. I didn't know it at the time, but when I found out, I thought this could be to my benefit because he could relate, one alcoholic to another. *Wrong!* He took me for $10,000 and did absolutely nothing except take my money, and I was in no condition to fight him. I could see I was being attacked again by the devil with situations I couldn't control.

I had an AA Sponsor and friends in AA that helped me through difficult situations. They honestly helped me more than the so-called Christian women I encountered in the food bank I volunteered for. I also knew I couldn't handle living in the house any longer because I was being threatened every time he got drunk. I made the mistake once again of thinking the police could help me—after all, I was at least 250 miles away from where Sharon lived, and it wasn't the same police department, but when I called the police for help, they showed up and told me he could threaten me and talk to me anyway he wanted to because that was his house. I was under attack once again by the devil, so I moved into a Motel 6 for a week, trying to figure out my next move. I was still working on my book, but my thoughts were all over the place, and it was very hard to focus. I once again called my ex-husband for help and asked him if I could come back to Maryland to finish writing my book. He said yes, so I called my wonderful friends from AA, and they helped me pack up my van, and my dog and we were on the road back to Maryland, with my ex-husband calling me every day for the next five days, asking me, "Are you up yet?" Some things never change, thank God!

Foreword

I am very blessed to have the Holy Spirit guide me and the gift of discernment to let me know right from wrong. God never leaves your side and never breaks his promises. You just can't make this stuff up, and I still have video and recordings to prove it. I made the decision to follow God's path for me, and he continued to show me he was with me all the way; I never walked alone. The moral of my story is, as broken as I was at the time, and through all my addictions, all my dumb mistakes—and I made some doozies—God still wanted to use me and anyone else who chooses to follow what he has planned for us, regardless of all the mistakes we make. Our God is a loving, forgiving God, and he hears our prayers. And remember, when you're walking with the Holy Spirit, it's "Father's house, Father's rules" and he can take all of our mistakes in life to help others. Don't ever think we're too broken or that God doesn't care, because he sure does—more than we will ever comprehend. Just look at me.

At the end of the day, this world is not getting any better—we can all see that. God knew what was going to happen, and he gave us a book (the Bible) warning his children. He also shared with us what we needed to do to inherit the kingdom of heaven and have eternal life. I joined AA, and the friendships I made in the program are invaluable to me, and because of God, my Holy Spirit, and being of sober mind, I am able to share my story with whoever wants to gain insight into mental illness, a narcissist's demons, injustice, and the goodness of God's grace.

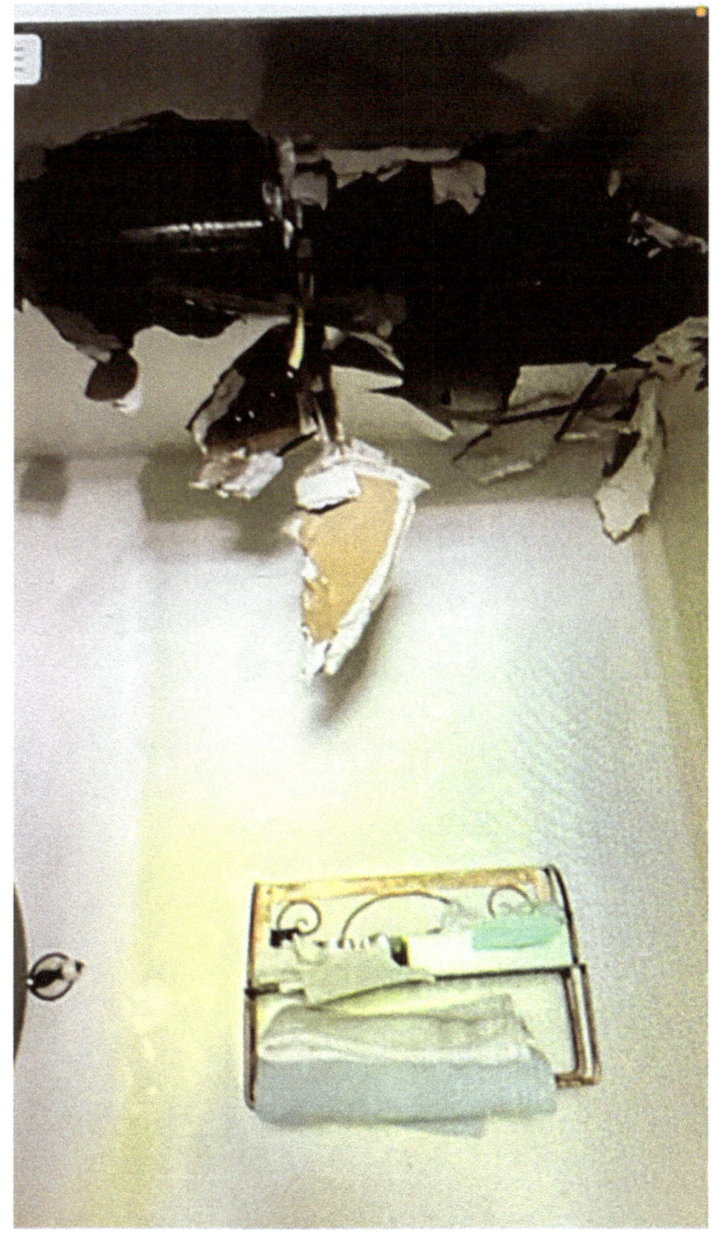

Incident Detail Report

Data Source: **Data Warehouse**
Incident Status: **Closed**
Incident number: **22-0010494**
Case Numbers:
Incident Date: **2/2/2022 15:25:38**
Report Generated: **12/5/2022 09:08:24**

Incident Information

Incident Type:	Structure	**Alarm Level:**	1
Priority:	CODE-F3	**Problem:**	STRUCTURE FIRE
Determinant:	69E01	**Agency:**	Ventura County Fire Department
Base Response#:	0410	**Jurisdiction:**	VNC West
Confirmation#:		**Division:**	Ojai Urban
Taken By:	Lam, Heather	**Battalion:**	Ojai Urban
Response Area:	013A	**Response Plan:**	STR 2018u LMT
Disposition:	CLEAR	**Command Ch:**	8 COMMAND 8
Cancel Reason:		**Primary TAC:**	9 TAC 9
Incident Status:	Closed	**Secondary TAC:**	10 VFIRE 26
Certification:		**Delay Reason (if any):**	
Longitude:	119251088	**Latitude:**	34446617

Incident Location

Location Name:		**County:**	Ventura
Address:	406 W Ojai Ave	**Location Type:**	
Apartment:	RM 00	**Cross Street:**	S RINCON ST/BRISTOL RD
Building:		**Map Reference:**	441-H7
City, State, Zip:	Ojai CA		

Call Receipt

Caller Name:	T-Mobile USA, Inc.		
Method Received:		**Call Back Phone:**	(805) 258-1900
Caller Type:		**Caller Location:**	12540 CREEK RD
Caller Address:		**Caller Location Phone:**	
Caller Building:		**Caller Apartment:**	
Caller City, State, Zip:		**Caller County:**	

Time Stamps / Elapsed Times

Description	**Date**	**Time**	**User**	**Description**	**Time**
Phone Pickup	2/2/2022	15:25:38			
1st Key Stroke	2/2/2022	15:25:38		**Received to In Queue**	00:00:14
In Waiting Queue	2/2/2022	15:25:52		**Call Taking**	00:09:10
Call Taking Complete	2/2/2022	15:34:48	Lam, Heather	**In Queue to 1st Assign**	00:00:10
1st Unit Assigned	2/2/2022	15:26:02		**Call Received to 1st Assign**	00:00:24
1st Unit Enroute	2/2/2022	15:27:09		**Assigned to 1st Enroute**	00:01:07.1
1st Unit Arrived	2/2/2022	15:29:24		**Enroute to 1st Arrived**	00:02:15.4
Closed	2/2/2022	16:10:19	Mobile1	**Incident Duration**	00:44:41

Resources Assigned

Unit	**Primary Flag**	**Assigned**	**Disposition**	**Enroute**	**Staged**	**Arrived**	**At Patient**	**Delay Avail**	**Complete**	**Odm. Enroute**	**Odm. Arrived**	**Cancel Reason**
ME21	Y	15:26:02		15:27:39		15:29:24			16:10:19			
B16	N	15:26:02	CLEAR	15:27:09		15:30:32			15:57:11			
B1	N	15:26:02	CLEAR	15:27:21					15:32:56			
MRE23	N	15:26:02		15:28:42					15:49:15			
MT5	N	15:26:02	CLEAR	15:27:14					15:32:51			
E22	N	15:26:02	CLEAR	15:27:42					15:32:57			
ME1	N	15:26:02	CLEAR	15:27:18					15:32:43			
ME2	N	15:26:02	CLEAR	15:27:19					15:32:44			

Personnel Assigned

Unit	**Name**
ME21	Gonzales, Tim (107385) - Fire Captain; Hopcus, Jesse (107900) - Fire Engineer; Zumpano, Michael (128610) - Fire Fighter
B16	Gutierrez, Israel (104840) - Fire Battalion Chief
B1	Manzano, Luis (21084) - Fire Battalion Chief
MRE23	Frailey, Austyn (130740) - Fire Fighter; Harrold, Ben (122007) - Fire Engineer; McHale, Tony (104921) - Fire Captain; Plum, Ryan (126650) - Fire Fighter; Romero, Jarrid (128606) - Fire Fighter
MT5	Briceno, Emmanuel (924176) - Fire Fighter; Kay, Jason (21241) - Fire Captain; Royston, Ryan (924178) - Fire Fighter; Westbrook, Michael (21998) - Fire Engineer
E22	Bacigalupo, Nick (127985) - Fire Engineer; Johnson, Ian (121606) - Fire Captain; Minadeo, Thomas (124946) - Fire Fighter
ME1	Brewer, Chad (21238) - Fire Captain; Comey, Kyle (23034) - Fire Engineer; Labarge, Graham (24531) - Fire Fighter
ME2	Foulke, Austin (23798) - Fire Fighter; Gray, Nicholas (24658) - Fire Fighter; Mitchell, Luke (22655) - Fire Captain

Caution Notes
No Caution Notes found

Permits
No Permit Information

Pre-Scheduled Information
No Pre-Scheduled Information

Transports
No Transports Information

Transport Legs
No Transports Information

Comments

Date	Time	User	Type	Conf.	Comments
2/2/2022	15:26:08	ZetronM25	Response		[1] 21 Alerted at 02/02/2022 15:26:08 for ME21
2/2/2022	15:26:11	ZetronM25	Response		[2] B10 Alerted at 02/02/2022 15:26:11 for B1
2/2/2022	15:26:17	ZetronM25	Response		[3] 23 Alerted at 02/02/2022 15:26:17 for B16,MRE23
2/2/2022	15:26:21	ZetronM25	Response		[4] 23 Alerted at 02/02/2022 15:26:21 for B16,MRE23
2/2/2022	15:26:25	ZetronM25	Response		[5] 23 Alerted at 02/02/2022 15:26:25 for B16,MRE23
2/2/2022	15:26:28	ZetronM25	Response		[6] 5 Alerted at 02/02/2022 15:26:28 for MT5
2/2/2022	15:26:31	ZetronM25	Response		[7] 22 Alerted at 02/02/2022 15:26:31 for E22
2/2/2022	15:26:34	ZetronM25	Response		[8] 1 Alerted at 02/02/2022 15:26:34 for ME1
2/2/2022	15:26:37	ZetronM25	Response		[9] 2 Alerted at 02/02/2022 15:26:37 for ME2
2/2/2022	15:26:46	HML	Response		[10] [ProQA Dispatch] Dispatch Level: 69E01 (HIGH LIFE HAZARD) Response Text: STR Problem Description: REPORTED BUILDING/STRUCTURE FIRE Chief Complaint: 69, CCText: Structure Fire
2/2/2022	15:26:46	HML	Response		[11] [ProQA: Key Questions] 1. HIGH LIFE HAZARD.
2/2/2022	15:27:24	HML	Response		[12] BLDG BEING EVACUATED
2/2/2022	15:27:49	HML	Response		[13] [ProQA: Key Questions] 2. Caller not inside bldg. 3. Multi-story: 2 4. No one trapped. 5. Fire loc: BATHROOM CEILING FIXTURE 6. Floor: 1ST FLOOR 7. No inj.
2/2/2022	15:28:08	KAF	Response		[14] Duplicate call appended to incident at 15:28:08
2/2/2022	15:28:42	KAF	Response		[15] BAY ALARM CALLED IN W ACTIVATION - ADVISED OF STR FIRE REPORT
2/2/2022	15:30:21	GMO	Response		[16] ME21 2 STY MULTI UNIT HOTEL NOTH SHOW ALARM SOUNDING // 2ND IN STG AT THE ENTRANCE AND PREPARE FOR WTR SUPPLY
2/2/2022	15:31:12	GMO	Response		[17] [Notification] B16 VCSO FOR TRAFFIC CONTROL ISOLATING OJAI AVE IN BOTH DIRECTIONS
2/2/2022	15:32:57	GMO	Response		[18] ME21 BURNED UP LIGHTING FIXTURE IN THE BATHROOM // CAN HANDLE WITH MRE23
2/2/2022	15:33:05	KAF	Response		[19] [Notification] VCSO REQ'D
2/2/2022	15:33:19	GMO	Response		[20] B16 CXL REQ FOR TRAFFIC CONTROL
2/2/2022	15:33:21	KAF	Response		[21] VCSO CXL'D

Address Changes
No Address Changes

Priority Changes
No Priority Changes

Alarm Level Changes

Date	Time	User	Change to Alarm
2/2/2022	15:26:02	MH	1

Activity Log

Date	Time	Radio	Activity	Location	Log Entry	User
2/2/2022	15:25:52		Incident in Waiting Queue			
2/2/2022	15:25:52		ANI/ALI Statistics		INT Insert:Feb 02 2022 15:25:38 / INT SendNP:Feb 02 2022 15:25:37 / WS RecvNP:Feb 02 2022 15:25:37 / WS Process:Feb 02 2022 15:25:52	HML
2/2/2022	15:25:52		SOP Updated		Updated SOP information is available	HML
2/2/2022	15:25:52		Waiting Pending Incident Time Warning		Waiting Pending Incident Time Warning timer expired	
2/2/2022	15:25:52		Problem Nature	406 W Ojai Ave	Incident problem nature changed from <Blank> to STRUCTURE FIRE	HML
2/2/2022	15:25:57		Remove Waiting Pending Incident Warning		Removing Waiting Pending Incident Time Warning timer expired	
2/2/2022	15:25:57		Incident in Waiting Queue Timer Clear			
2/2/2022	15:25:58		UserAction		User clicked Initial Assign	MTH
2/2/2022	15:25:59		Initial Assignment		The following unit(s) is (are) recommended for assignment: ME21 (00:00:58),B16 (00:01:15),B1 (00:19:54),MRE23 (00:04:43),MT5 (00:22:37),E22 (00:04:27),ME1 (00:16:35),ME2 (00:19:30)	MTH
2/2/2022	15:26:02	B16	DISP	406 W Ojai Ave	Response Number (0411)	MTH
2/2/2022	15:26:02	ME1	DISP	406 W Ojai Ave	Response Number (0417)	MTH
2/2/2022	15:26:02	ME21	DISP	406 W Ojai Ave	Response Number (0410)	MTH
2/2/2022	15:26:02	ME2	DISP	406 W Ojai Ave	Response Number (0418)	MTH
2/2/2022	15:26:02	E22	DISP	406 W Ojai Ave	Response Number (0416)	MTH
2/2/2022	15:26:02	MT5	DISP	406 W Ojai Ave	Response Number (0415)	MTH
2/2/2022	15:26:02	B1	DISP	406 W Ojai Ave	Response Number (0412)	MTH
2/2/2022	15:26:02	MRE23	DISP	406 W Ojai Ave	Response Number (0413)	MTH
2/2/2022	15:26:02		Incident Command Channel	406 W Ojai Ave	Command Channel 8 COMMAND 8 has been added.	MTH
2/2/2022	15:26:02		Incident Primary TAC Channel	406 W Ojai Ave	Primary TAC Channel 9 TAC 9 has been added.	MTH
2/2/2022	15:26:02		Incident Alternate TAC Channel	406 W Ojai Ave	Alternate TAC Channel 10 VFIRE 26 has been added.	MTH
2/2/2022	15:26:08		Read Comment	406 W Ojai Ave	Comment for incident 017 was marked as read.	INT_BOOTSTR

2/2/2022	15:26:21	ME2	Update Vehicle Destination	SEAWARDAVE	Update Unit Destination To 406 W Ojai Ave, APT RM 00	HML
2/2/2022	15:26:21	ME21	Update Vehicle Destination	MONTGOMERYST	Update Unit Destination To 406 W Ojai Ave, APT RM 00	HML
2/2/2022	15:26:21	ME1	Update Vehicle Destination	VENTURAAVE	Update Unit Destination To 406 W Ojai Ave, APT RM 00	HML
2/2/2022	15:26:21	B16	Update Vehicle Destination	MARICOPAHWY	Update Unit Destination To 406 W Ojai Ave, APT RM 00	HML
2/2/2022	15:26:21	MRE23	Update Vehicle Destination		Update Unit Destination To 406 W Ojai Ave, APT RM 00	HML
2/2/2022	15:26:21	B1	Update Vehicle Destination	SEAWARDAVE	Update Unit Destination To 406 W Ojai Ave, APT RM 00	HML
2/2/2022	15:26:21	MT5	Update Vehicle Destination	HARBORBLVD	Update Unit Destination To 406 W Ojai Ave, APT RM 00	HML
2/2/2022	15:26:21	E22	Update Vehicle Destination		Update Unit Destination To 406 W Ojai Ave, APT RM 00	HML
2/2/2022	15:26:35		Premise History Access		Premise History Viewed	KAF
2/2/2022	15:26:39		UserAction		User clicked Exit/Save	KAF
2/2/2022	15:26:46		ProQA	406 W Ojai Ave	ProQA determinant sent	HML
2/2/2022	15:26:50		UserAction		User clicked Exit/Save	ALW
2/2/2022	15:27:09	B16	ENR	406 W Ojai Ave, APT RM 00	Responding From = MARICOPAHWY.	6021
2/2/2022	15:27:14	MT5	ENR	406 W Ojai Ave, APT RM 00	Responding From = HARBORBLVD.	CN04
2/2/2022	15:27:17	ME2	ENR	406 W Ojai Ave, APT RM 00	Responding From = SEAWARDAVE.	CN09
2/2/2022	15:27:18	ME1	ENR	406 W Ojai Ave, APT RM 00	Responding From = VENTURAAVE.	CN22
2/2/2022	15:27:19	ME2	ENR	406 W Ojai Ave, APT RM 00	Responding From = SEAWARDAVE.	CN09
2/2/2022	15:27:21	B1	ENR	406 W Ojai Ave, APT RM 00	Responding From = SEAWARDAVE.	CNB1
2/2/2022	15:27:24		UserAction		User clicked Exit/Save	MTH
2/2/2022	15:27:39	ME21	ENR	406 W Ojai Ave, APT RM 00	Responding From = MONTGOMERYST.	6627ME
2/2/2022	15:28:02		Incident Late		Active incident marked as late	
2/2/2022	15:28:08		Duplicate Call Warning		Duplicate Call Warning - New call appended to incident	KAF
2/2/2022	15:28:43		UserAction		User clicked Exit/Save	KAF
2/2/2022	15:28:57		UserAction		User clicked Exit/Save	ALW
2/2/2022	15:29:24	ME21	OS	406 W Ojai Ave, APT RM 00		6627ME
2/2/2022	15:29:43		UserAction		User clicked Exit/Save	MES
2/2/2022	15:30:32	B16	OS	406 W Ojai Ave, APT RM 00		6021
2/2/2022	15:32:23		UserAction		User clicked Exit/Save	MTH
2/2/2022	15:32:31		UserAction		User clicked Exit/Save	MES
2/2/2022	15:32:43	ME1	AVAIL	406 W Ojai Ave, APT RM 00	Unit Cleared From Incident 22-0010494	CN22
2/2/2022	15:32:44	ME2	AVAIL	406 W Ojai Ave, APT RM 00	Unit Cleared From Incident 22-0010494	CN09
2/2/2022	15:32:51	MT5	AVAIL	406 W Ojai Ave, APT RM 00	Unit Cleared From Incident 22-0010494	CN04
2/2/2022	15:32:56	B1	AVAIL	406 W Ojai Ave, APT RM 00	Unit Cleared From Incident 22-0010494	CNB1
2/2/2022	15:32:57		UserAction		User clicked Exit/Save	MTH
2/2/2022	15:32:57	E22	AVAIL	406 W Ojai Ave, APT RM 00	Unit Cleared From Incident 22-0010494	6606
2/2/2022	15:33:05		Notify Comment		(Response Viewer)	
2/2/2022	15:33:23		UserAction		User clicked Exit/Save	KAF
2/2/2022	15:34:47		UserAction		User clicked Exit/Save	BRO
2/2/2022	15:34:48		UserAction		User clicked Exit/Save	HML
2/2/2022	15:46:14		UserAction		User clicked Exit/Save	ALW
2/2/2022	15:46:54		UserAction		User clicked Exit/Save	ALW
2/2/2022	15:47:00		UserAction		User clicked Exit/Save	ALW
2/2/2022	15:49:15	MRE23	AVAIL	406 W Ojai Ave, APT RM 00	Unit Cleared From Incident 22-0010494	GMO
2/2/2022	15:57:11	B16	AVAIL	406 W Ojai Ave, APT RM 00	Unit Cleared From Incident 22-0010494	6021
2/2/2022	16:10:19	ME21	AVAIL	406 W Ojai Ave, APT RM 00	Unit Cleared From Incident 22-0010494	6627ME
2/2/2022	16:10:20	ME21	Response Closed	406 W Ojai Ave, APT RM 00	Response Disposition: CLEAR	6627ME

Edit Log

Date	Time	Field	Changed From	Changed To	Reason	Table	Workstation	User
2/2/2022	15:25:38	Call_Back_Phone		(805) 258-1900	(Response Viewer)	Response_Master_Incident	FPDVEN01DIS201	HML
2/2/2022	15:25:38	Address	(Blank)	12540 CREEK RD	New Entry	Response_Master_Incident	FPDVEN01DIS201	HML
2/2/2022	15:25:38	Agency Name		Ventura County Fire Department	(Response Viewer)	Incident	FPDVEN01DIS201	HML
2/2/2022	15:25:38	Call Back Phone		(805) 258-1900	(Response Viewer)	Incident	FPDVEN01DIS201	HML
2/2/2022	15:25:39	Jurisdiction		VNC West	(Response Viewer)	Response_Master_Incident	FPDVEN01DIS201	HML
2/2/2022	15:25:39	Division		Ojai Urban	(Response Viewer)	Response_Master_Incident	FPDVEN01DIS201	HML
2/2/2022	15:25:39	Battalion		Ojai Urban	(Response Viewer)	Response_Master_Incident	FPDVEN01DIS201	HML
2/2/2022	15:25:39	Response_Area		013A	(Response Viewer)	Response_Master_Incident	FPDVEN01DIS201	HML
2/2/2022	15:25:39	ResponsePlanType	0	0	(Response Viewer)	Response_Master_Incident	FPDVEN01DIS201	HML
2/2/2022	15:25:39	Address	12540 CREEK RD	406 W Ojai Ave	Entry Selected/Returned from GeoLocator	Response_Master_Incident	FPDVEN01DIS201	HML
2/2/2022	15:25:39	City		Ojai	Updated City	Response_Master_Incident	FPDVEN01DIS201	HML
2/2/2022	15:25:39	Latitude	0	34446617	Entry Selected/Returned from GeoLocator	Response_Master_Incident	FPDVEN01DIS201	HML
2/2/2022	15:25:39	Longitude	0	119251088	Entry Selected/Returned	Response_Master_Incident	FPDVEN01DIS201	HML

2/2/2022	15:25:42	AddressUpdateNeeded	False	True	from GeoLocator Wrapper generated update	Response_Master_Incident	FPDVEN01VRSOSTSSADMIN
2/2/2022	15:25:52	Problem		STRUCTURE FIRE	(Response Viewer)	Response_Master_Incident	FPDVEN01DIS201 HML
2/2/2022	15:25:52	Caller_Name		T-Mobile USA, Inc.	(Response Viewer)	Response_Master_Incident	FPDVEN01DIS201 HML
2/2/2022	15:25:52	Admin		46 C12 RED	(Response Viewer)	Incident	FPDVEN01TWS2 ECHO
2/2/2022	15:25:52	Air to Ground		11 VNC A/G	(Response Viewer)	Incident	FPDVEN01TWS2 ECHO
2/2/2022	15:25:53	Pickup_Map_Info		441-H7		Response_Transports	FPDVEN01DIS201 HML
2/2/2022	15:25:53	Map_Info		441-H7		Response_Master_Incident	FPDVEN01DIS201 HML
2/2/2022	15:26:02	Command Channel		8 COMMAND 8	(Response Viewer)	Incident	FPDVEN01DIS210 MTH
2/2/2022	15:26:02	Primary TAC Channel		9 TAC 9	(Response Viewer)	Incident	FPDVEN01DIS210 MTH
2/2/2022	15:26:02	Alternate TAC Channel		10 VFIRE 26	(Response Viewer)	Incident	FPDVEN01DIS210 MTH
2/2/2022	15:26:08	Field_Data		CHANTICO HOTEL	Location Info:	Response_User_Data_Fields	FPDVEN01DIS201 HML
2/2/2022	15:26:08	Unread Comment	False	True	(Response Viewer)	Incident	FPDVEN01VINT1 INT_BOOTSTRAP
2/2/2022	15:26:21	Apartment		RM 00	(Response Viewer)	Response_Master_Incident	FPDVEN01DIS201 HML
2/2/2022	15:26:46	Determinant		69E01	(Response Viewer)	Response_Master_Incident	FPDVEN01DIS201 HML
2/2/2022	15:26:46	EMD_Used	0	1	(Response Viewer)	Response_Master_Incident	FPDVEN01DIS201 HML
2/2/2022	15:26:46	CIS_Used	0	null	(Response Viewer)	Response_Master_Incident	FPDVEN01DIS201 HML
2/2/2022	15:26:46	Pro Qa Case Number Fire		1429017	(Response Viewer)	Incident	FPDVEN01DIS201 HML
2/2/2022	15:29:30	CIS_Used	0	null	(Response Viewer)	Response_Master_Incident	FPDVEN01DIS201 HML
2/2/2022	15:29:30	Pro QA Termination State Code		C	(Response Viewer)	Incident	FPDVEN01DIS201 HML
2/2/2022	15:29:30	ProQATerminationStateCode		C	(Response Viewer)	Incident	FPDVEN01DIS201 HML

Custom Time Stamps
No Custom Time Stamps

Custom Data Fields

Description	**Data**	**User**
Admin	46 C12 RED	ECHO
Air to Ground	11 VNC A/G	ECHO
Location Info:	CHANTICO HOTEL	HML

Attachments
No Attachment

Incident Report

Entries in this report are intended for the sole use of the Ventura County Fire Protection District. Estimations and evaluations made hereon represent "most likely" and "most probable" cause and effect determinations by fire district personnel. Any representation as to the validity or accuracy of reported conditions outside the Ventura County Fire Protection District is neither intended nor implied. Due to the variability in estimating property and content value and loss, the Ventura County Fire Protection District takes no position of such damages and, as a consequence, this report may be referenced by a $0 loss estimate in the fire district's database. Without an approved release, any and all confidential information protected by law was redacted or removed.

The Custodian of Records for Ventura County Fire Protection District has generated the enclosed incident information from its computer database. This is a certified copy of the information contained in District records as of the date this report was printed.The contents of this report are current as of that date and may not contain all information relevant to the incident. As warranted, after further review of the matter, additional information may be added to the report by appropriate fire district personnel.

Incident Number: 220010494 | Date Issued: 12/05/2022 09:20:40

Issued by Custodian of Records Office | Page 1 of 2

Ventura County Fire Protection District, 165 Durley Ave, Camarillo, California 93010
VCFPD complies with the U.S. Fire Administrations' National Fire Incident Reporting System (NFIRS)
Code index found at http://www.nfirs.fema.gov/documentation/reference/

VENTURA COUNTY
FIRE PROTECTION DISTRICT
INCIDENT REPORT 220010494

1. BASIC

Incident Date	Incident Number	Exposure	Station	Location Type
02/02/2022	220010494	000	21 - Ojai	1 Street address

Address
406 W OJAI Ave

Apt/Suite/Rm
RM 00

City, State & Zip
Ojai, CA 93023

Cross Street
[None selected]

Incident Type
445 Arcing, shorted electrical equipment

Aid Type
N None

Mutual Aid Department

Their Incident Number

Alarm Time	Arrival Time	Control Date/Time	Last Unit Cleared Time
02/02/2022 15:25:38	02/02/2022 15:29:25		02/02/2022 16:10:20

Action Taken
87 Investigate fire out on arrival

Detector (confined fires)
U Undetermined

Property Use
449 Hotel/motel, commercial

Fire Related Casualties

Fire Service Deaths	0	**Fire Service Injuries**	0
Civilian Deaths	0	**Civilian Injuries**	0

Jurisdiction Unincorporated(County) **Responsibility Area** [None Selected]

Remarks

ME21 on scene of a 2 story hotel room with nothing showing and manual pull alarm on. Upon investigating room #00 found light residual smoke from a burnt out motor on a bathroom vent with the vent obvious burnt and still hot on thermal imager on the first floor. ME21 crew quickly had to check for possible extentionand cleared the drywall around the vent. There was minor heat markd to wood and insulation but no fire. MRE23 was used for smoke ejection and alarm was solenced.
Hotel mananger on scene contactyed maintenance and alarm company for pull alarm reset and damge repair.
Overhaul damage was limited to drywall.

2. APPARATUS/PERSONNEL

Apparatus ID	Apparatus Type	Use	Number of People
E22	11 Engine	Suppression	3
B16	92 Chief officer car	Other	1
MRE23	11 Engine	Other	5
ME21	11 Engine	Suppression	3

Employee Name
Timothy P Gonzales
Jesse J Hopcus
Michael D Zumpano
Israel T Gutierrez
Anthony M McHale
Benjamin J Harrold
Ryan M Plum
Jarrid M Romero
Austyn J Frailey
Ian P Johnson
Thomas J Minadeo
Nicholas D Bacigalupo

12/05/2022 09:20:40 Page 2 of 2 FDM PIR LR - 1/31/13

Record Type Requested: FIRE INVESTIGATION REPORT - Not all fires will have a Fire Investigation Report. Depending on the incident complexity and other factors a report may not be completed for weeks or months

Other:

Incident Number:

Incident Date: 02/03/2022
Incident Time: 09:10 am

Incident Type: electrical fire

Address/Location: 406 WEST OJAI AVE
Cross Street (if known): chantico inn
City/Community: ojai

Requestor: Dina Harris
Phone: (805) 538-4362
Fax:
Email: areyoureadynow@icloud.com
Mailing Address:
114 jennifer drive

Indian Head, Maryland 20640

Bexar County ESD 10
6658 E. HOUSTON ST.
San Antonio, TX 78220
210 661 3144
rhogan@bcesd10.org
Printed: 02/28/2023 15:58:38
Number of Pages: 4

Incident Report
2020-0004518 -000

Basic	
Alarm Date and Time	09:45:07 Sunday, December 20, 2020
Arrival Time	09:50:43
Controlled Date and Time	
Last Unit Cleared Date and Time	11:41:24 Sunday, December 20, 2020
Response Time	0:05:36
Turnout Time	0:00:00
Completed	Yes
Reviewed	Yes
Fire Department Station	167
Shift	A
Incident Type	111 - Building fire
Aid Given or Received	1 - Mutual aid received
Mutual Aid Department	CFD-Converse Fire Department
Action Taken 1	11 - Extinguish
Casualties	No
Apparatus - Suppression	2
Personnel - Suppression Personnel	6
Property Loss	$1,000.00
Contents Loss	$500.00
Property Value	$1,000.00
Contents Value	$500.00
Detector Alerted occupants	U
Property Use	419 - 1 or 2 family dwelling
Location Type	Address
Address	7138 Walnut Trace
City, State Zip	UBC, TX 78239
District	BC 10 FD-2
Directions	7138 Walnut Trace
Latitude	29.519571
Longitude	-98.347995
Map Page	553E7

Situation	
Initial Dispatch Code	SF
Final Dispatch Code	SF

Additional Mutual Aid Agencies	
Aid Department	Universal City Fire Department
Aid Department	Windcrest Fire Department

Person Involved - wood, tyler, -	
Involvement Code	REP
Last Name	wood, tyler
First Name	-
Street Address	
Phone	3015422774

Fire

Bexar County ESD 10
6658 E. HOUSTON ST.
San Antonio, TX 78220
210 661 3144
rhogan@bcesd10.org
Printed: 02/28/2023 15:58:38
Number of Pages: 4

Incident Report
2020-0004518 -000

Fire	
Structure Type	1 - Enclosed building
Number of Residential	1
Area of Origin	21 - Bedroom - < 5 persons; included are jail or prison
Heat Source	13 - Arcing
Item First Ignited	81 - Electrical wire, cable insulation
Cause of Ignition	3 - Failure of equipment or heat source
Contribution To Ignition 1	00 - Other factor contributed to ignition

Structure	
Status	2 - In normal use
Floor of Origin	1
Stories Above Grade	1
Building Length	10
Total Square Feet	10
Fire Spread	2 - Confined to room of origin
No Flame Spread	1
Detector Presence	1
Detector Type	1 - Smoke
Detector Power	U - Undetermined
Detector Operation	2 - Detector operated
Detector Effectiveness	1 - Alerted occupants, occupants responded
AES Presence	3

Apparatus - CH166		
Apparatus ID	CH166	
Response Time	0:08:44	
Turnout Time	0:00:00	
Apparatus Dispatch Date and Time	09:47:07	Sunday, December 20, 2020
En route to scene date and time	09:47:07	Sunday, December 20, 2020
Apparatus Arrival Date and Time	09:55:51	Sunday, December 20, 2020
Apparatus Clear Date and Time	11:40:57	Sunday, December 20, 2020
Apparatus priority response	Yes	
Number of People	2	
Apparatus Use	Suppression	
Apparatus Type	92 - Chief officer car	
First Arriving Unit	Yes	
Personnel 1	BCFA90022 - Hogan, Robert Position: FC	
Personnel 2	147 - Gonzalez, Sergio Position: FF	

Apparatus - E167		
Apparatus ID	E167	
Response Time	0:12:32	
Turnout Time	0:00:00	
Apparatus Dispatch Date and Time	09:47:04	Sunday, December 20, 2020
En route to scene date and time	09:47:04	Sunday, December 20, 2020
Apparatus Arrival Date and Time	09:59:36	Sunday, December 20, 2020

Page 2 of 4 Printed: 02/28/2023 15:58:38

Dina Harris

Bexar County ESD 10
6658 E. HOUSTON ST.
San Antonio, TX 78220
210 661 3144
rhogan@bcesd10.org
Printed: 02/28/2023 15:58:38
Number of Pages: 4

Incident Report
2020-0004518 -000

Apparatus - E167	
Apparatus Clear Date and Time	11:26:10 Sunday, December 20, 2020
Apparatus priority response	Yes
Number of People	4
Apparatus Use	Suppression
Apparatus Type	11 - Engine
Personnel 1	164 - Amezquita, Christopher Position: LT
Personnel 2	122 - Herrera, Miguel Position: FF
Personnel 3	157 - Silva, Joshua Position: FF
Personnel 4	271 - Montero, Joseph Position: PFF

Authority	
Reported By	164 - Amezquita, Christopher 16:06:28 Sunday, December 20, 2020
Officer In Charge	- ,
Reviewer	110 - Faktor, Gary L 07:50:09 Monday, December 21, 2020

Narratives	
Narrative Name	Call Summary
Narrative Type	Incident
Narrative Date	15:54:28 Sunday, December 20, 2020
Author	164 - Amezquita, Christopher
Author Rank	LT
Author Assignment	1
Narrative Text	At 0945 hours on Sunday December 20, 2020 we were dispatched to a building fire. Two units were assigned to this incident. Six personnel responded. We arrived on scene at 0950 hours and cleared at 1141 hours. The incident occurred at 7138 Walnut Trace, UBC in District BC 10 FD-2. The local station is 167. The general description of this property is 1 or 2 family dwelling. The primary task(s) performed at the scene by responding personnel was extinguishment. Mutual aid was received on this incident.

The involved structure is described as an enclosed building. The building was occupied and operating. "Bedroom for less than five persons" best describes the primary use of the room or space where the fire originated. This building has one story above ground. The fire occurred on the first floor. The fire was confined to the room of origin. "Arcing" best describes the heat source that caused the ignition. Failure of equipment or heat source caused the ignition. The use, or purpose of the material that was first ignited was "electrical wire, cable insulation".

The building was equipped with smoke detectors. The detector(s) operated properly. The detector(s) alerted the occupants and the occupants responded.

The estimated property loss on this incident was $1,000. The estimated content loss was

Bexar County ESD 10
6658 E. HOUSTON ST.
San Antonio, TX 78220
210 661 3144
rhogan@bcesd10.org
Printed: 02/28/2023 15:58:38
Number of Pages: 4

Incident Report
2020-0004518 -000

Narratives

$500. The estimated property value was $1,000. The estimated content value was $500.

E167 responded responded for a structure fire. Prior to arrival AC 145 was on location and assumed command. Per the size up we were noified that there was smoke coming out of the alpha bravo side . A second update stated there was fire coming out of the eves of the home. When we arrived on location we were the primary engine and went offensive. There was fire located in the alpha bravo room in the right corner near the window. There were books a lamp and an amplifier on fire with aproximately three foot flames. We searched for extension in the room of origin and and completed a primary search. The home was then ventilated since the entire home was filling with smoke. a portion oof ceiling was pulled to check for extension. A section of sheet rock was also removed to look for extension. Natural and mechanical ventilation was used for the call.

Alarm number 0004518 has been assigned to this incident.

End of Report

Page 4 of 4 Printed: 02/28/2023 15:58:38

It took us five days to get home and learn the valuable lesson God had taught me. I am now over a year clean and sober and got rebaptized. I attend a Bible-based church and worship on the Sabbath. I can't thank my God enough for pulling me out of the darkness and into the light.

> Ephesian 6:12 For we do not wrestle against flesh and blood, but against the rulers, against the authorities, against the cosmic powers over this present darkness, against the spiritual forces of evil in the heavenly places.

Printed in the USA
CPSIA information can be obtained
at www.ICGtesting.com
LVHW011046271023
762204LV00019B/740